6/98

6/98

A PHOTOGRAPHIC GUIDE TO
BUYING &
SELLING HORSES

A PHOTOGRAPHIC GUIDE TO
BUYING &
SELLING HORSES

All the information you will need to ensure that you buy and sell
successfully, and how to spot the potential risks and pitfalls

VANESSA BRITTON

David & Charles

Picture acknowledgements
The author and publishers would like to thank the following for supplying illustrations for this book:

Derek Croucher: p29 (top); Kit Houghton: pp10, 16, 17 (top), 21, 65 (top), 66 (btm), 67 (btm), 70 (top), 73 (top), 76 (top), 83 (top), 84 (btm), 89 (top), 92 (btm), 127, 129, 130, 131, 139; D. C. Knottenbelt, p90 (btm); Bob Langrish: pp9 (btm right), 14 (both), 28 (top), 65 (btm), 66 (top), 69 (btm), 72 (top two), 73 (btm), 77 (top), 82 (btm), 83 (btm), 84 (top), 85 (top), 86 (top, btm right), 93 (top), 94 (top, btm right); Anthony Reynolds: pp8, 9 (top three), 12 (left), 15 (top), 17 (btm), 28 (btm), 29 (btm), 31, 35, 36, 45, 46 (right), 49 (left two), 53, 54 (middle), 55 (all), 70 (btm), 88 (top), 95 (btm), 101, 104 (both), 105 (left), 109 (top), 110 (top), 116, 121 (btm), 125, 128, 137, 147 (both), 148 (btm), 150; Colin Vogel: pp102, 109, 110, 113. The line illustration on p26 is taken from An Illustrated Guide to Horse Tack by Susan McBane (David & Charles), and the one on p97 from The Complete Performance Horse by Colin J. Vogel (David & Charles).
The publishers would also like to thank Colin Vogel for the text and captions on pp58-9.

A DAVID & CHARLES BOOK

First published in the UK in 1997

A catalogue record for this book is available from the British Library.

ISBN 0 7153 0377 5

Book design by Visual Image
Printed in Italy by Milanostampa SpA
for David & Charles
Brunel House Newton Abbot Devon

CONTENTS

1
BEFORE PURCHASE

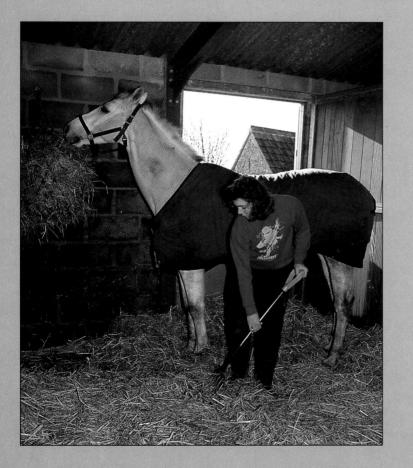

FIRST CONSIDERATIONS

Buying a horse is not a decision to be taken lightly, for horse ownership is a responsibility that is fraught with uncertainties and expense. Good horses are usually expensive to buy, but this sum can become fairly insignificant when compared to the costs involved in owning and keeping a horse. While owning your own horse may be the realisation of a childhood dream, it is crucial that you should consider carefully every aspect of horse ownership as it will change your life in many ways. Apart from a mortgage or a car, your horse may be the most expensive thing you ever buy, yet, unlike a house or a car, it cannot be paid for and then forgotten about until you feel like a change. In becoming a horse owner you are committing yourself to your horse's upkeep and care. You are also responsible for your horse's happiness and well-being, so perhaps the first pre-purchase consideration is not whether the horse is right for you, but are you right for any horse?

Your initial reaction to this question will probably be, 'Of course I am!' However, consider the points given in the box below, and then ask yourself that question again.

If, having considered all of them carefully, you still feel that buying a horse is the right thing for you, then go ahead because you are sure to make a very good owner. Conversely, if you feel you are not really ready for ownership, do not despair. There are several other options, such as sharing, loaning, or working for rides, and these are explained further on pages 17–21. Having taken the decision to buy, the next step is to evaluate all the costs involved so that you can be sure that now is the right time for you to do so. Providing for your horse is dealt with fully in Chapter 2.

POINTS TO CONSIDER BEFORE BUYING A HORSE

Do you have a suitable place to keep a horse? If all you can offer is a ramshackle shed and a patch of weeds, then don't even think of buying one. This pony was rescued by the International League for the Protection of Horses

1 Apart from the initial cost, can you truly afford the upkeep of a horse, remembering that you may have to find veterinary fees and other unforeseen costs at short notice?

2 Do you have enough time to see to your horse's needs adequately, or enough money to pay someone else to do so for you?

3 Do you have suitable, permanent accommodation and grazing, or do you know of a vacant place in an appropriate livery yard?

4 Do you have the necessary knowledge and skill to care for your horse's needs, or the back-up of experienced friends?

5 Do you have someone experienced enough and willing to care for your horse if you are ill?

6 Have you really thought why you want a horse of your own? Wouldn't an hour's hacking at the weekend be enough?

CHOICE OF HORSE

What sort of horse is right for you? Well, it is definitely not the most beautiful nor the first one you see. It is well known that once someone has decided to buy a horse for the first time, they are often in such a hurry that almost any horse seems to please them. Do yourself a huge favour by not going to look at any horses until you have a clear picture in your mind of the sort of horse that would be right for you. The idea of owning the next Milton might seem attractive to all of us, but unless you ride as well as John Whitaker, perhaps you should think again. At all times, remind yourself that you cannot afford to make a mistake, so be guided by your head, not your heart. Even better would be to let an experienced person guide you. Before you go to look at any horse you must establish a few boundaries, otherwise you will not be the first person to have set off in search of a 15.2hh part-bred horse only to return with an unbroken New Forest colt which you felt you just had to 'rescue'. You should consider the factors given in the box below.

MAKING THE RIGHT CHOICE

What do you want to do with your horse or pony? Will its size matter? Remember, in children's classes the height of the pony is often related to the age of the rider.

TYPE AND CONFORMATION

What activities are you interested in? Do you intend to show, or is jumping ability a more important consideration? A cob is not going to make a Grand Prix dressage horse, while an Arab is never likely to prove a staid hack.

Who else is going to ride your horse? If it is intended as a family horse, choose with great care for all concerned, bearing their experience and ability in mind.

Where are you going to keep the horse? A native pony will thrive outdoors, while a Thoroughbred will need rugs and a stable.

AGE AND TEMPERAMENT

How experienced are you? A young horse will need an experienced rider.

How long do you want the horse for? A younger horse might suit you if you are thinking of selling on fairly quickly.

How much can you afford to pay? An older horse is likely to be cheaper than a younger one of comparable quality.

Do you have the experience to deal with a horse of questionable temperament? A horse will take advantage of you if you are nervous, or novice: thus jogging can become pulling, nappines rearing, and grumpiness develop into kicking and biting.

HEIGHT

How tall are you? If you are tall, you will require a tall horse.

Will anyone else be riding your horse? Do you need a horse that will also suit someone shorter or taller than yourself?

COLOUR AND SEX

Do you have a personal preference? No one colour is any better than another, but some people simply do not like a certain one, eg chestnut mares are often thought to be over-excitable. It is true that greys are more difficult to keep clean.

Do you have any thoughts of breeding in the future? If so, perhaps a mare would be a good choice for you.

CHOOSING YOUR FIRST HORSE

As a first-time buyer, choosing the right horse is of the utmost importance. This may seem an obvious statement, but it may surprise you to know that many people buy horses which are simply not suitable for them. Your first horse needs to be one that will improve your confidence, both as a rider and an owner. This does not mean that the horse needs to be a real old plod who wouldn't put a foot wrong but, rather, that its character and manners are well within your capability to handle without fear. The sort of horse that you will need will depend upon your abilities, likes and dislikes. Take the advice of your instructor at the outset, and value that opinion, even if it includes something you do not really want to hear.

When buying a pony for a child, go for reliability and safety. Ponies can be very strong and quick to take advantage of small children. Your child should enjoy riding, not dread it! So don't go for good looks; go for a happy combination of child and pony.

There is no such thing as a 'perfect' horse, but there *is* such a thing as the right horse for you. In the USA, Quarter Horses are a popular choice for first-time owners as they have a docile, easy-to-manage temperament. However, there is also a growing use of American Sport Horses which are a Thoroughbred/draught cross (usually Clydesdale or Shire). Similarly, in the UK, horses which have some native blood in them, such as Welsh Cob or Dartmoor, or 'common blood' (a term which loosely covers draught-type horses such as Shires, Percherons, Clydesdales, Suffolk Punches and Irish Draughts), are said to be a better choice for a first-time owner as they are likely to be more amenable than a Thoroughbred or an Arab, for instance.

However, the breed of horse is not as important as the right temperament, and if enough time and effort are spent in looking, then a truly suitable horse can be found, regardless of breed, colour or sex. Many people are opposed to buying a mare as a first-time horse, blaming them for being skittish when in season. However, many mares are not 'mareish' and even if one is, if she works well at all other times there is little cause to dismiss her. Mares are often said to be more perceptive than geldings where novice or nervous riders are concerned. Accepting that there is no such thing as a perfect horse, notice should be taken of the prospective owner's individual faults, idiosyncrasies, likes and dislikes, and the amount of tact they might need to ensure they get the best out of any horse.

A Quarter Horse stallion; notice the enormously well developed muscles of his forearm! Although powerfully built, the Quarter horse is renowned for its amenable character and is increasingly popular in the USA with first-time owners. However, it has not become established in the UK as a popular breed, probably because the native horses and ponies fit the same requirement: they are easy to manage, physically hardy, and come in different shapes and sizes to suit all sorts of shaped riders!

NO HORSE IS PERFECT, BUT IT MUST BE RELIABLE

When looking for a first-time horse, whether it is for yourself or for your child, use these simple points as a guideline:

1 Look for a horse that has proved itself to be what you want. A horse that is 100 per cent safe in traffic and genuinely good in all respects is worth far more to you at this stage than any 'potential star'.

2 Decide upon the minimum age of horse you feel you can cope with and stick to that decision.

3 Draw up a list of your strengths and weaknesses and match those of any potential purchase to it. An area in which you are lacking must be one of the horse's strongest points. For example, if you have not had much experience of handling horses, as opposed to riding them, the horse must be a true gentleman or lady to handle.

4 Don't fall in love with the first horse you see. Always remember that the wrong horse will cost just as much to keep, if not more, than the right horse with which you will also have a lot of fun.

5 Buying the wrong horse may put you off horses for life, so do go about it in a practical, and wholly sensible way.

6 Don't be too prejudiced by colour or slight personal preferences; you might have to wait a long time until the ideal horse comes along, and in the meantime many perfectly suitable ones may have passed by.

7 Everyone becomes an expert when it is someone else's horse, so only take the advice of a person you truly trust to be honest with you.

For most people, a horse that is 100 per cent reliable in traffic is worth far more than one with Olympic potential

A competition horse

Buying a competition horse requires a totally different set of rules from the first-time purchase. Those buying a competition horse should have a good few years' experience behind them, and should know instinctively what they are looking for. Unless the horse is being selected as a potential show horse, for a specific category, there are often fewer constraints as to what may be suitable. A showjumper need not be a strapping 16.2hh Warmblood if it can jump well, for instance. Although you may have a preconceived idea of what you would really like, it is ability that counts, and while exquisite movement or fantastic athletic ability may seem like a big deal to start with, be careful that it doesn't blind you to a horse's other faults. Most professionals soon adopt the opinion that they couldn't care less what a horse looks like, or how it behaves in the stable if it is a winner. However, heed a word of warning here: they may not have to deal with the horse day in, day out, but you will. If a horse's behaviour or problems are so bad that they start to make you late for work, or you arrive in a bad temper, your performance together may soon start to suffer as a result.

A horse for the more mature rider

If you are coming into riding or horse ownership late in life there are certain things you should consider. Firstly, what sort of horse could you cope with? You may feel that your age is not

The more mature rider is probably less keen to take risks for fear of incurring injury and is therefore looking for a horse which is sensible and reliable, straighforward to 'do', traffic- and fright-proof, and experienced in the rider's preferred activity

a consideration, but it is a plain fact of life that we all slow down as we get older, that our reactions are not as quick, and somehow things don't always fall into place as easily as they used to. Couple this with the fact that you probably have more responsibilities and commitments than you used to, and that if you fall off you may be hurt more easily, and you can begin to see that owning a horse for the first time in later life needs quite a bit of thought.

This is not to say that you should not buy a horse, simply that you need to make doubly sure you choose the right one. Do you simply want to hack out, or does long distance riding or showing interest you, for example? It takes a long time to build a partnership with a horse, so you won't want to go on struggling for years with a horse with which you just don't 'click'.

Know exactly what you want you horse to do. Thus if you want to go showjumping you would look for exceptional natural jumping ability in a youngster, and you would expect an older horse to have a good record in competition

Low-budget horses

The mention of 'low-budget' horses immediately provokes visions of horses hobbling around on three legs, or of ones that buck you off every time you sit on them. There is no such thing as a 'bargain' horse, so caution is the only approach if a horse is described in this way. There are some perfectly good horses that can be obtained more cheaply than normal, but in all cases you should be aware of what you are taking on and should satisfy yourself that you have the necessary skills to do so. The old adage 'beggars can't be choosers' does apply here, but sometimes it is better to have no horse than a cheap one that may cost you dearly in the end.

Problem horses

You are strongly advised to think very carefully indeed before you buy a problem horse. Many people will always advise you against it – although really, everything depends upon your own strengths and weaknesses. For instance, you may not be the world's greatest rider but you may have an empathy with horses that will enable you to straighten out a behavioural problem. Similarly, if you are a very confident rider, you may be able to sort out problems that were caused by a frightened or inexperienced rider.

When considering a problem horse, always try to find out as much of its history as possible, so that you can assess its problems down to the last detail. Many things *can* be straightened out as the majority of problems have their roots in past owners' mistakes and inefficiencies. However, do think twice about taking on a confirmed rearer or a horse which habitually naps or bolts, as such traits can be extremely difficult to conquer once established and could result in both you and the horse being badly hurt or even killed.

Other types of problem horse include those with health conditions such as chronic obstructive pulmonary disease (COPD) or stringhalt. If such a condition will not detract from what you intend to do with the horse, and you are fully aware of how to manage it, then you can proceed confidently with the purchase, providing you are happy with the asking price – which should, of course, reflect the fact that there *is* a problem.

A horse for a rider with a disability

Few people with disabilities have a horse of their own but there is much to recommend this, providing they have the means to care for it properly. Most riders with disabilities ride through the Riding for the Disabled Association groups, and therefore ride the horses and ponies in a riding school situation. When looking at a horse as a potential purchase for this sort of activity, certain criteria must be met. In particular, it is well known that a rider with a disability does *not* need a disabled horse.

Temperament is the very first thing to consider. The horse should have a quiet disposition as those which are high-spirited rarely settle to this special kind of work, and they can often be unpredictable. This should not be confused with a horse which is initially frisky, but settles to its job well. This is just a sign of good health. On the other hand, a horse that is sluggish or appears lifeless is of no real value either. The horse or pony must be forward-going and straight-moving, with a happy outlook. It must lead easily and walk or trot rhythmically, be willing to carry out its duties, and it should stand perfectly still when required.

The horse's character must also be evaluated. 'Cheeky' should not be interpreted as 'naughty'. A cheeky pony may do its work extremely well, and it is all to the good if it enjoys life. As long as it does its job willingly, it may even provide inspiration for the rider. A pony which does not have any apparent character of its own does not help its rider to form a bond and, consequently, does not motivate the rider, which is one of the main aims of the Riding for the Disabled Association.

Riding is a hugely successful therapeutic activity for people with disabilities: their delight and pleasure at being in such close contact with the ponies is rewarding in itself, and they nearly always make rapid progress not only in what they learn to do physically, but also in confidence, courage and in learning to trust others

Young horses

Young horses can often be bought more cheaply than older ones which have had some training. Horses in this category include:

- weanlings, which come straight from their mothers and require expert handling;
- youngsters up to about three years old which have not yet been backed;
- horses of four or five years old which have been backed and turned away.

Are you considering a weanling (above) or may be a three-year-old at the start of his training (left)? Ask yourself if you have both the knowledge and the set-up to handle young horses. Any youngster, and in particular a weanling, is bound to be frightened, insecure and impressionable in a new environment, and rough or ignorant handling could ruin his confidence and his attitude to humans for ever

Unless bred from top-class stock and specifically for a certain discipline, weanlings can be purchased for about a quarter of the price of an average riding club-type horse. However, they do require skilful handling and knowledgeable feeding and management. If you have the necessary skills, you can gain a great deal of satisfaction from 'producing' your own horse, but lack of experience only brings heartache, so do be truthful with yourself before buying a weanling.

Youngsters of up to three years of age will probably have had some handling (the more so the older they are), but you will need to go through the backing and training process yourself, unless you intend to send the horse

away to be backed professionally. If you are an experienced rider, have worked around horses for a good while, have the necessary facilities or can hire them, and have some willing help, you will more than likely find the experience both worthwhile and satisfying. If you don't have these advantages then think again. While there is much to commend sending a horse away to be backed professionally, unless money does not matter you are wasting your time because for the cost involved you would be better off buying a ready-schooled horse on which you can have fun straightaway.

Finally, you can acquire horses of four to five years old which have been backed and turned away, but in which

case you will need to provide all their training and schooling. This can be immensely satisfying if you have the ability to do this work and is less fraught than buying a slightly younger horse which is yet to be backed. With such a horse you can be quite successful. Regular lessons from a qualified instructor will help to keep you on the right path, so budget for these along with the initial purchase price. Do be aware, however, that being able to ride a fairly well balanced, well mannered riding-school horse is not at all the same as riding a youngster. Youngsters can be spooky and unpredictable, and you must be able to deal with everything that happens and know that you are competent enough to win every battle.

Older horses

An older horse is far more suitable if you are less experienced, but there are other drawbacks. A horse in its mid- to late teens may have accumulated veterinary complications, especially in the back and legs, which, although they may not prevent it from being ridden, will require regular treatment or specialist care. Additionally, an older horse may need to be kept in, or have the benefit of more rugs or special feed. However, such costs may be within your reach when offset against the reduced initial purchase price, so making the horse affordable to you. When considering the purchase of an older horse, be sure to give each individual a fair assessment. While you might not have twenty years of service ahead of you, an older horse can still provide years of pleasure and you cannot beat this sort for giving confidence and a feeling of safety. Providing you can cope with the idea that, at the end of its life, you will still be responsible for the horse and will have to deal with putting it down, there is much to recommend elderly horse ownership for nervous or older riders or for children who are not particularly bold, all of whom will treat the animal with consideration.

A steady, reliable temperament and outlook are most important considerations when buying a horse or pony for a rider with disability, and in this respect an older animal generally has the maturity and experience which make it ideal for this rôle

An older horse can provide a great deal of pleasure, but it may be more difficult to keep it in good condition

Horses retired from a competitive life

Very often horses are retired early from competitive disciplines for a variety of reasons, perhaps because they do not have the ability to make it to the top at the level at which they competed, or because they appear not to enjoy their work, or simply because they have suffered an injury which prevents them from competing any longer. Such horses may be fine for hacking, breeding or general riding club work and may therefore find a home with a less ambitious owner, often for a fraction of the cost of their initial purchase. It is well known that failed racehorses sell for three noughts less the second time they are sold, and this is also true for most other spheres of equestrianism. Nevertheless, as with other cheaper horses, be sure that you

know what you are taking on. If you don't have great ambitions, such a horse could be a godsend. Usually it will have been handled continually and efficiently, so its manners should be good and it is likely that it will be far less worried by travelling, hustle and bustle or a move to a new yard. Unlike youngsters, such horses have seen it all before. Do be aware, however, that the training a racehorse has received may make it quite unsuitable to hack quietly across open fields, and retraining may be required.

Rescued horses

Some welfare groups and charities allow the re-homing, or fostering of many of their horses. However, they do have strict standards as to who will make a suitable 'foster' owner. You will need to have a suitable, safe place in which to keep the

A retired racehorse may prove to be a bargain but be sure you know what you are taking on

horse, either at home or at a reputable livery yard, and you will have to show evidence of your competence as a potential owner, and also assure them that your financial situation will provide for a horse. Rescued horses often need a lot of tender loving care, so if you work long hours, forget it. Also bear in mind that you will have the responsibility of restoring your horse's faith in human kind, so taking on such a horse is a commitment in itself. The advantages are that you will be helping the charity or organisation from which the horse came, and that you can rest assured that should you no longer be able to provide for the horse, it will always have a safe 'home' to return to.

ALTERNATIVES TO OWNERSHIP

What can you do if, having really thought about purchasing your own horse, you find you simply cannot afford one, even on a budget? There are a number of ways to get low-cost, or even totally free rides, but what you don't have in the way of hard cash you will have to make up for by means of commitment and riding ability. There are many busy horse owners who would like to see their horses exercised more but who shy away from letting other people ride them through fear of their horses being, at best, upset by careless riding or, at worst, ruined by a total lack of riding ability. The onus is on you to show that you are both capable, and sincere.

To begin with you need to start work on acquiring the label of being 'available'. You can do this by attending local equestrian events and establishments, such as:

- shows
- riding schools
- livery yards
- Riding for the Disabled centres
- welfare organisations.

Being seen around and making yourself useful will show others that you are committed to horses, and if you are allowed to ride at such places in return for your help, they will also be able to judge your skills for themselves. You could also post a notice in your local tack shop or feed merchant, or place a small advertisement in the local paper offering your services to exercise other people's horses.

If you wish to ride other people's horses, what you don't have as hard cash you will have to make up for through commitment, and by showing people what you are capable of doing, and more important, prepared to do. For example, a great deal of work is involved in running even the small local show, which may involve clearing fences away and generally fetching and carrying. Perhaps even closer to home, jobs around the yard such as mucking out may be lacking in glitz and excitement, but they still have to be done, day in, day out. Show you are available and reliable and people will be well disposed towards you

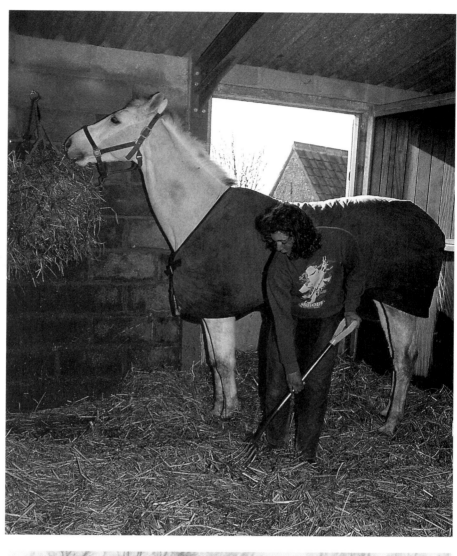

EXERCISING AND WORK FOR RIDES

There are two benefits to riding someone else's horse. Firstly, you will not have to bear the usual costs of horse ownership and, secondly, you can get a feel of what it is like to be responsible for a horse if you are considering buying one of your own later on.

Many owners will be only too happy to have your help, but you must be able to back up what you say about your riding skills with evidence of competitive successes, examination or test passes, or oral references from people who are happy to vouch for your ability. Certain times of the year are busier than others, such as the hunting season and the build-up to competitions. If you are a good rider and are available quite often, you will probably find yourself in great demand.

Riding schools are a great place to start if you are less experienced. They will often let you ride in exchange for help with mucking out, tack cleaning and the like. Such work can be quite demanding, but you will have the benefit of learning a great deal. There really is no better place to start if you are thinking about buying your own horse at a later date, and there is no better way of earning free lessons than by doing something you really enjoy.

If you can't afford to keep a horse of your own, then consider helping at your local riding school; jobs such as cleaning tack, mucking out and grooming may be tedious, but it is all good experience for you and in return for your hard work and enthusiasm you may be allowed cheaper, or even free rides

SHARING

Buying a horse requires quite a substantial outlay, even for the basic, everyday riding horse. Couple this with all the upkeep fees and we are talking about a considerable sum of money – so what can be done to ease the financial burden? One idea that may be a practical solution for two people who get on well is a share scheme. This will either involve jointly purchasing a horse, or one existing owner agreeing to share his/her horse with a second party. Do be aware, however, that share schemes can make enemies of the best of friends, so from the outset, draw up an agreement in writing so that both parties know where they stand, as this is sure to prevent many disputes in the future.

As one horse is not likely to be the 'ideal' type for both parties wanting to share a horse, such a scheme will always be a compromise. However, while there are disadvantages, such as not being able to ride whenever you feel like it, or to go to a show you want to, there are also advantages, of which sharing the costs and chores are the most beneficial. If the two sharers are of the same size, then there is little problem regarding the size of the horse, and the normal buying procedure can be followed – but what if one is 6ft (1.8m) tall, weighing 13 stone (83kg), and the other 5ft (1.5m) tall, weighing 8 stone (51kg) as many husband/wife partnerships are? The taller, heavier rider will feel very underhorsed on a little horse which is ideal for the smaller, lighter rider, who, in turn, would feel very over-

horsed on an ideal horse for the former. In such situations you need a short-legged horse with a big body, such as a cob which is a type rather than a breed. Whilst show cobs do not exceed 15.1hh, a good all-round fun sort can be about 15.2hh and will suit many different types of rider.

Another way of sharing is to allow your horse to become a working livery. This means that a riding school will be able to use it for hacks and lessons, charging you less for its livery in return. This may work well if your horse is not too sensitive to be ridden by other riders of mixed ability, and if you don't become frustrated, or even jealous at the sight of others riding it. In reality, however, most people soon wish they had their horse to themselves again.

GUIDELINES ON SHARING

If you are the loanee, you should only compete in the more arduous disciplines if the owner if fully cognisant as to what it involves

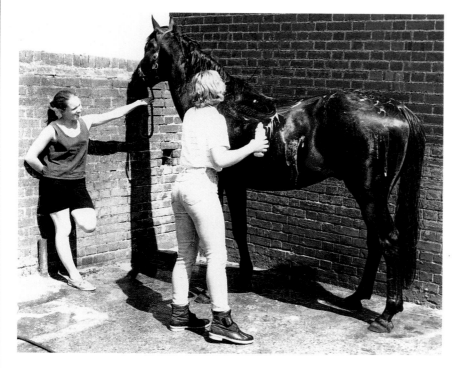

Many jobs can be shared of course – including the grotty ones!

An agreement should take into account the following matters:

1. How much each party should pay towards the purchase and upkeep. While this may seem obvious in a 50/50 agreement, one party may wish to have far more access to the horse, in which case a 25/75 agreement may be more suitable.

2. Times should be set down as to when each party may have use of the horse, bearing in mind that weekend access is likely to be most desirable to both parties.

3. Who does what regarding everyday care? Are chores taken in turns daily, or is one party responsible for doing the morning shift and the other the evening shift, for instance?

4. If you are sharing a competition horse, it is essential to work out a programme for everyone at the start of the season. Perhaps having two riders will confuse the horse, and so cause him to perform less well than you might expect: so what do you do? Perhaps one is happy to groom and exercise, and leave the competition riding to the other? Or one to do the summer events, and the other to compete in the winter? And does shared ownership affect a horse being able to take part in qualifying competitions? And, what is most relevant if both riders are keen to compete, be sure to work out a holiday for the horse: he should not be expected to perform until he is worn out and sick of it!

5. Should the horse be sold, who gets what; and what if one partner wants to pull out of the arrangement?

It may also help to look at the conditions for loaning a horse (see page 20), as certain of those may also apply.

LOANING

If you simply do not have the initial money required to buy a horse but can afford the upkeep costs on a regular basis, then loaning is the answer. 'Loaning' is simply another term for 'borrowing' and while in nearly all cases you will be expected to take on the maintenance costs, a few owners do agree to share some of the expenses. Horses for loan are often referred to as 'meat for manners' – the owner provides the 'meat'; you provide the 'manners'. This arrangement works well if you want a horse for only a short period of time, perhaps through the competition season, or if the owner wants to loan his horse for only a short period of time. Sometimes horses are offered on loan for an indefinite period, perhaps because the owner can no longer afford to keep the horse, but wishes always to have a link with it. Be careful if considering this option and ensure that you agree what is to happen to the horse if you find that you can no longer keep it. There have been cases where the owner will not agree to sell the horse but nor will he/she take it back. While the situation can be resolved through the courts, you may find yourself stuck with the horse and all its upkeep for many months or even years.

Again, it is in both parties' interests to draw up an agreement at the outset. The purpose of drafting any agreement is to pre-empt potential problems and so safeguard the interests of owner and borrower who are then totally aware of what they have, or have not, agreed to. Should the other party not wish to enter into a written agreement, then you might ask yourself why?

As the borrower, you should be aware of the importance of such 'terms of use', as you are likely to be held responsible for even the slightest degree of neglect, even more so if you were doing something with the horse that was not agreed or previously put down in writing.

You should also pursue what will happen if the horse needs a major new purchase, such as a rug or a saddle. You may consider buying such items yourself if they are for your benefit, but do remember that a saddle should be well

LOAN AGREEMENTS

A loan agreement should cover every point you can think of, including:

ON THE OWNER'S PART

1 The disclosure of any known health problems from which the horse suffers.

2 The right to remove the horse should there be evidence of mistreatment.

3 That date at which the loan period will cease, if it is not an indefinite loan.

4 Providing the horse is being well treated, that it will not be taken back prior to this date, unless agreed between both parties beforehand in writing.

5 Terms of use of the horse, for example: hacking only; the level of competition permitted; breeding.

6 Who is responsible for insurance.

7 That the owner will retain any papers, such as a registration or freeze-branding certificates, pertaining to the horse, so that there can be no disputes of ownership.

8 What tack is usually worn by the horse and what may be permitted for use.

9 Reasonable visiting rights of the owner, which must be set down in writing.

10 The length of a trial period.

ON THE LOANEE'S PART

1 To call the veterinary surgeon without delay whenever necessary.

2 To feed and clothe the horse with all due care.

3 To maintain any tack or clothing also loaned in good order.

4 To ensure that no mistreatment occurs, whether due to lack of funds, wilful neglect or carelessness.

5 To agree to the terms of use.

6 To agree not to pass the horse on to a third party without the owner's consent.

7 To return the horse on the agreed date.

8 Only to use the horse for the activities as laid down in the terms of use.

9 Not to move the horse to new premises without the owner's permission, and to agree the owner's right to inspect the new premises.

10 To insure the horse, if it is decided that this is not the owner's responsibility.

11 Not to use any tack which is not permitted.

12 To inform the owner of any change of circumstances which may affect the horse.

fitted to the particular horse that wears it, so it is not something you can drop onto the back of the next horse you might become involved with. Discuss with the owner whether they will agree to share the costs of such purchases, or at least to buy the items from you should you all part company – and remember to get such an assurance in writing. When you agree to loan or take possession of a horse you should be fully aware that you are entering into a contractual relationship with the other person. Such a contract is valid in law and, whether it is a verbal one or written down, you are bound by it.

Providing you start on such an informed basis, loaning can be most enjoyable. While fairly common in the UK, and becoming increasingly popular, loaning or leasing is not particularly usual in the USA where generally it only applies to people leasing a proven competition horse for a year.

LEASING

Leasing differs from loaning in that you may be (but are not always) expected to pay a 'lump sum' for the use of the horse, as well as providing for its upkeep. Leasing is more common in cases where the horse has a fairly high value, perhaps because it is a talented competition horse or of high-class breeding stock. Leasing may be attractive where, for instance, the outright purchase price would preclude ownership, while leasing may provide the less wealthy enthusiast with a chance to own a contender for a major international competition. The lease fee should be considerably lower than an outright purchase price and, in fairness, should reflect such factors as the value the lessee may add to the horse during the lease period. This arrangement may work extremely well between a talented young rider and a non-competitive, but nevertheless enthusiastic owner or, more likely, breeder of quality horses. Free leases are a fairly common arrangement where breeders wish to retain their stock for breeding but want someone else to 'put money on the horse's card' in the meantime, thus raising its stud value. In return, the lessee has all the pleasure of competing with the horse as if it were his/her own.

A lease usually runs for a set number of months or years, to be agreed by lessor and lessee. The benefit of leasing a horse is that you may have use of a particular horse, or type of horse that you simply could not afford to buy. The drawback is that you will have had all the upkeep costs, plus the initial cost, with nothing to show for it at the end of the lease period.

In order that you know what to expect, be sure to ask the owner for a guide to the horse's usual upkeep fees, including how often and how much it is fed and shod, for example. You will then have some guide to the expenses involved and can budget for them accordingly. Should the horse have any health problems, you should be made aware of them before agreeing to lease the horse. If such information is not forthcoming, you must ask the owner outright. If he or she does not seem willing to discuss this matter, you should become suspicious and reconsider the whole idea.

If you are considering a long-term lease agreement, it may be wise to have the horse vetted, something to which a sincere owner should not object. You should also ask to have the horse on a trial period of at least a month, but more suitably two, before totally committing yourself to a lease agreement. During this time you can ensure that you are compatible with the horse and that it does not have any faults or vices of which you were not informed. Also be aware that while some horses can be perfectly well behaved at home, they may change character when moved, so do allow the horse a period in which to settle in, thus making it a truly fair trial on your part.

For those embarking on a long-term lease arrangement, or who intend to take part in more strenuous activities such as hunting, jumping or Pony Club games, it may be advisable to have the horse or pony checked over by a vet to be sure that it is sufficiently sound in wind and limb to cope with the work you have in view for it

LEARNING FROM LOANING

Vicki and Richard Davies had to go to work abroad for twelve months, so they asked Samantha and Colin Rhodes, the proprietors of a local livery yard, to look after their in-foal mare until their return the following year. Knowing that the mare would foal while they were away, they asked Samantha and Colin to look after her and the foal as if they were their own. On their return from abroad Vicki and Richard would take the foal and leave the mare with Samantha and Colin as 'payment' for caring for the mare and foal during their absence.

The mare foaled the following spring, without complications, and Samantha and Colin named the TB/Irish Draught filly Holly. They started to get a little concerned as they had heard nothing from Vicki and Richard since they had gone. As it turned out they never returned. When Holly became a five-year-old Samantha and Colin broke her in to be ridden. A few months later, having gone through a really rough period in their marriage, they decided to divorce, and so had to sell their many horses and ponies. However, they did not feel able to sell Holly, so 'gave' her to Jane, their friend.

After a month of having Holly, Jane decided she wanted to buy her, and wanted to sort the whole arrangement out with a proper agreement. By this time Samantha and Colin had split up, and as Samantha had moved away, Jane asked Colin for the owners' address so she could sort it out with them, before spending out to have Holly properly schooled. Colin asked Jane to pay him something for the five years he had kept Holly, but Jane felt this was nothing to do with her and said if he put her in touch with the owners she would sort out the purchase with them. Colin agreed to find and pass on their address, but in fact he never did.

Jane paid for Holly to be schooled and undertook all the financial implications of her upkeep and management for five years. She then went through a difficult period when she lost her grazing, was working full time, and had a baby to look after, so she allowed Holly to go out on loan for a year. The loan then ended, but friends of the loanee's wanted to buy Holly. Having had no contact with either Samantha or Colin for over five years Jane decided the best thing to do was to sell Holly to a good home. As she saw it, Holly had been given to her and she had covered all her costs for five years; in her mind the mare had become her property.

A further five years later (by which time Holly was fifteen years old) Jane met Samantha's stepdaughter Joanne (Colin's daughter) who showed a sudden and unexplained interest in the whereabouts of Holly. Jane's mother was extremely ill at the time, so she simply gave Joanne the address of the loanees, who informed her that Jane had sold the horse for £900.

Two weeks later Jane received a letter from Samantha's solicitor demanding £900 for selling something that did not belong to her. Jane replied with a lengthy letter explaining exactly what had happened. She never heard another word from any of the parties involved.

MORAL *For both the person loaning and the loanee: make sure you draw up a proper written agreement so that both parties are aware of the exact 'terms' of any loan agreement.*

Additionally, if the horse or pony is given as a 'gift', whereby it passes into the ownership of the new keeper without any money changing hands, ensure that this is put down in writing as such, and signed by both the previous and the new owners.

2
PROVIDING FOR YOUR HORSE

WHERE TO KEEP THE HORSE?

Having bought your horse you have both a moral and a legal responsibility to satisfy all of its physical and psychological needs. Complete commitment is required, which demands regular feeding, grooming, riding, health care and attention to the horse's social needs, all of which are essential to its well-being.

Before you even think about looking for a horse, the first practical consideration is where you will keep it and how much this will cost. Opinions differ as to what constitutes a suitable environment for a horse, but the first thing to consider is whether your horse will be better off stabled or at grass.

There is no doubt that most horses will benefit from living out of doors most of the time, providing they have adequate shelter, food and company. While in the field they are able to exercise themselves, which may relieve you of the necessity of daily exercise should this prove difficult due to other commitments. However, a horse living out of doors will still need to be checked over twice a day and, where appropriate, fed to a regular routine.

During foul weather or when your horse is being ridden regularly, or competed often, stabling may prove to be more convenient for you. However, a stabled horse needs to be fed, watered, mucked out and exercised properly or its health will suffer, so weigh up the time required for this against the time you have available before you decide to stable your horse for much of the time.

Eventually you will find a system that suits your own particular circumstances. This is most likely to work itself into a combined system where your horse is stabled part of the time but is otherwise turned out.

Having decided upon the most suitable environment for your horse, you can then begin to consider where you will keep it.

At home

This is only a feasible option if you have at least two acres of land per horse, and a safe building of a generous size that will accommodate it. Generally, the rule

is that a stable of 10 x 10ft (3 x 3m) is acceptable for a small pony, 10 x 12ft (3 x 3.5m) for a larger one, with the minimum size for a 16hh horse being 12 x 14ft (3.5 x 4.25m). Additionally, you will have to take fencing and paddock maintenance costs into consideration. Post-and-rail fencing is still the safest option, but it is not cheap even if you erect the fencing yourself. Another consideration when keeping your horse at home is that of companionship. As herd animals, horses are happiest when in the company of their own kind, so a field and stable companion will be necessary. This may be an older, retired horse or an

Whether you keep your horse at home or at livery, at some point he will need to be stabled – perhaps the weather is terrible, he may be ill, you may want to keep him clean for a show or a day's hunting. The costs involved are obviously higher, but they must be taken into consideration

If you intend to turn your horse out, post-and-rail fencing is undoubtedly the best and safest option, although it is expensive both to put up and to maintain. In the long term, however, the accumulative cost of setting up and maintaining decent fencing and a sound, big enough stable is probably less than paying a weekly livery

unsound one. Whilst such a horse may cost very little in terms of initial outlay, do not forget that it, too, will need a stable, rugs, feed and maybe veterinary care. Ideally, and if facilities permit, you could take in a livery which will also help with the financial costs. This could be on a DIY basis if you have little time, or full livery if you can care for the horse alongside your own.

While the initial cost of setting up a suitable stable and paddock for a horse at home may seem quite high, in the long term it works out cheaper than having to pay livery costs. Additionally, of course, your horse will be available whenever you want to ride, and fairly safe as you can keep a check on it at most times of the day and night.

Livery

If you do not have the necessary facilities at home in which to keep a horse, then you will need to find a suitable livery yard. How much this will cost will vary depending on the type of livery, the yard's facilities and the area in which you live. For instance, livery is cheaper in farming communities than it is in industrial areas. However, do check out a yard very carefully before deciding to keep your horse there, as standards vary enormously. The types of livery which are generally available include:

- Do-it-yourself (DIY): where *you* see to all your horse's needs. The cost of a stable will be included if your horse requires a stable. If your horse is to be kept out full-time, then this livery may be termed as 'grass livery'. NB: If your horse is kept solely at grass livery, ensure that there is a stable with lighting into which it may be brought in cases of emergency. Costs for grass livery (1996) may be anything between £10 and £20 per week, with the stable costing you up to £10 more per week if for your sole use.

- Half livery: where the yard looks after your horse's physical needs, but you ride and perhaps groom it. Costs will vary between £30 and £50 per week.

- Full livery: where the yard takes complete care of your horse, including exercise and grooming. Costs will vary between £50 and £80 per week.

Where people board their horse in the USA depends very much on the district. In heavily built-up areas where owners commute to work, horses are usually kept in large livery yards. But further out in the countryside there is a more even split between people boarding their horse and keeping it at home. It is far more common to board horses in the USA than in the UK, and the concept of people getting up at 5am to 'do' their own horse at 5 am before setting off to the office doesn't really exist.

COSTS OF MAINTENANCE

Equipment for the horse

Whatever option you choose with regard to environment, you should be aware of both the expense of upkeep and the demands a horse will make on your time. As well as basic livery fees, you must also budget for vetting at the time of purchase; transport home and to and from shows; feeding and bedding (if these are not included in your livery costs); farriery; vet-erinary care; lessons; insurance; and equip-ment. Get quotes on all of these expenses before you buy your horse so that you can see how much it is going to cost you on a weekly basis. If you are going to have to cut corners in order to keep a horse, you should seriously consider whether this is the right time for you to be buying one.

When you are deciding what equip-ment is necessary for your horse, there are three rules to bear in mind:

- It is quality that counts.
- Simplicity is the key.
- Buy from a reputable saddlery or ask a knowledgeable person to check the saddlery for you.

Too many people buy things that are simply not necessary at the outset, so the following sections on tack, rugs, yard equip,ment and first-aid require-ments list the essentials.

TACK

If, at the time of purchase, you are not able to buy the horse's own tack (providing, of course, that it is worth buying), then you will have to buy it yourself from a saddlery or from a rep-utable supplier of secondhand equip-ment. Ask the previous owner what the horse is used to, particularly as regards bits and girths, so that you may avoid unnecessary purchases. Good quality tack is an investment but as we have implied, you need not buy new. Remember, 'it is quality that counts' and a used, but good quality piece of tack is always better than an inferior new one.

Costs for saddlery vary enormously. As a guide (1996), you might expect to pay between £7.50 and £15 for a head-collar; up to £80 for a new leather bridle, and around £350 to £700 for a new leather saddle. Second-hand leather tack can cut these prices in half, and so can synthetic tack. Synthetic tack has improved vastly since its introduction and it does allow a wide choice of items at very reasonable prices. It is also very easy to keep clean.

If you are unsure what to buy, be guided by your saddler who should have a craftsman's crest, or other emblem proving his respectability, prominently on display. In the UK this is the Society of Master Saddlers' crest. Such a saddler should also be happy to come out and fit a saddle to your horse, as correct fitting is of paramount impor-tance to your horse's comfort and to your own safety.

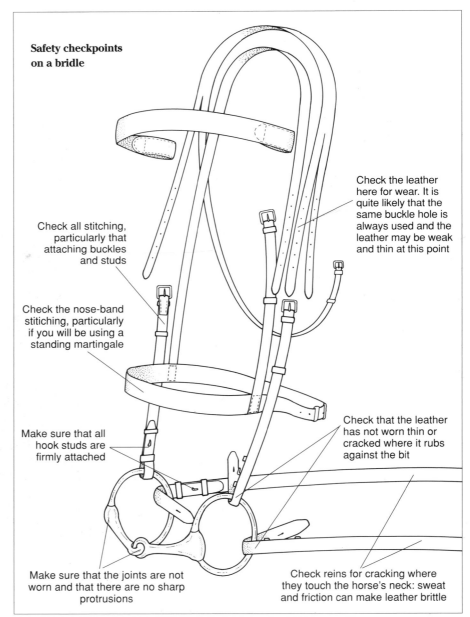

Safety checkpoints on a bridle

Check all stitching, particularly that attaching buckles and studs

Check the nose-band stitiching, particularly if you will be using a standing martingale

Make sure that all hook studs are firmly attached

Make sure that the joints are not worn and that there are no sharp protrusions

Check the leather here for wear. It is quite likely that the same buckle hole is always used and the leather may be weak and thin at this point

Check that the leather has not worn thin or cracked where it rubs against the bit

Check reins for cracking where they touch the horse's neck: sweat and friction can make leather brittle

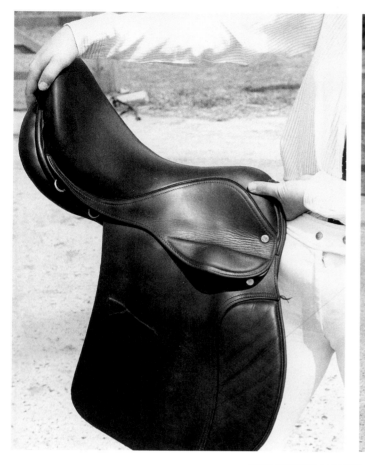

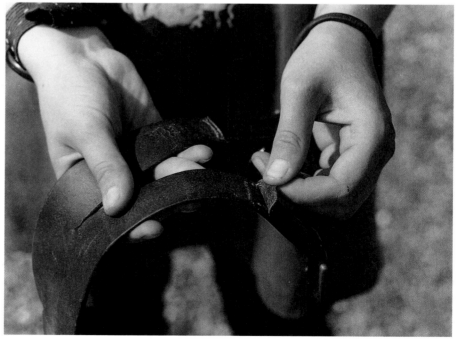

(above) Check the waist of the saddle by holding it as pictured, and pulling upwards; any movement or undue bend in this area will indicate damage to the tree

(above right) Test the front arch for rigidity: if it moves and 'spreads' the tree is almost certainly cracked. Also check that the padding on the underside is not too flat; if it is, the pommel arch is almost bound to press on the withers

Obviously the stitching on a girth should be double-checked; also the leather where it curls round the buckle – this is often a weak spot. On an Atherstone girth the leather tends to split where it divides at each end; the one pictured is just starting to do this; by the holder's thumb

RUGS

Numerous types of rug are now available, so make sure you know what you are buying. A New Zealand or turnout rug will probably be required for when your horse is turned out in winter, while a stable rug will be needed when indoors. To fit well, any rug should be properly shaped to folow the line of the horse's back; it will then right itself and be less likely to rub, or to slip when he shakes or rolls. It is best fastened by surcingles which are sewn or clipped to the rug and cross under the belly, rather than the traditional roller which causes direct pressure on the spine and invariably slips. It should come well forward of the withers, well back over the root of the tail, and be deep enough to come just below the elbow and stifle. In addition you may need a sweat rug, a summer sheet and a travelling rug. Rugs come in various different materials, and this is reflected in their cost. Again, you can buy used rugs but these are not always widely available. Initially you can expect to spend at least £150 on just a stable and turnout rug.

YARD EQUIPMENT

How much yard equipment you need depends on whether you keep the horse at home or at livery. At home, mucking-out and yard-sweeping implements are esssential: these include a four-pronged fork for straw stables (with a long enough handle or mucking out will make your back ache!) and/or a shavings fork for a deep litter bed; a skip and skipping out rake; a yard broom (plastic lasts longer) and a spade for keeping the yard surface neat and tidy, and sweeping out the stable; a *capacious* wheelbarrow, otherwise you are constantly having to trundle over to the muck-heap and empty it – the plastic variety are lighter and will spare your poor old back; and plenty of buckets. An old enamel sink serves well as a manger because it is big, it has smooth rounded edges and it can't be tipped over; or you can buy plastic feeding mangers which hook on the door. You will also need a haynet or two even if there are built-in hay-racks in the stable (when travelling; or you may need to wet the hay by immersing the net in water).

FIRST AID

The first-aid kit is an item often ignored, forgotten about or badly managed: it should, however, be considered essential. It should be readily available (not locked in the tack-room cupboard and no one knows where the key is); it should be reviewed and updated every month (mouldy powder and dressings damaged by mice have no curative value); and everyone likely to be involved with the horse should know how to use its contents (a thick layer of Kaolin will not relieve mud fever). Make sure your kit contains the items depicted: this should enable you to carry out *basic* emergency treatment. This might involve, for example, controlling bleeding when you would bandage a non-stick wound dressing and a gamgee pad firmly over the wound; or cleaning a wound, when you might use fresh water and gamgee swabs, and then apply antiseptic powder.

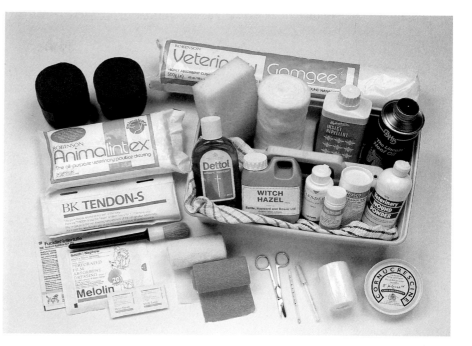

GROOMING KIT

You will certainly need a full grooming kit: starting with the hairier type of horse, you will need a plastic curry comb (there are two or three varieties with different width teeth) and a dandy brush to knock the mud off body and legs; also the dandy brush is often the only one which will get through the thicker, more unruly sort of mane and tail. For finer coats, and those that are clipped, you will need a soft body brush; use this on a finer mane and tail, too, because the dandy brush will pull out and damage finer hair – that of, say, an Aras or a Thoroughbred – and make it look straggly and thin.

At some point you are bound to want to wash off stable stains, or even to wash the whole horse: have a water brush and sponges for this, and a sweat-scraper to remove the excess water from the body hair. A wide-toothed mane comb will tease out the worse tangles, though don't use the smaller, close-toothed comb for this job because it will pull the hair out by the roots – indeed, this is the one to use for mane-pulling. No grooming kit is complete without a hook-pick, either. A hessian 'glove' to strap up a good shine, and hoof oil as a finishing touch – and you are ready for anything!

Equipment needed for the rider

A hard hat is the most essential piece of any rider's kit. Under section 218 of the UK *Highway Code*, children under 14 must, as a legal requirement, wear an approved safety helmet and fasten it securely; but whatever country you live in, this is a sensible precaution whether it is a legal requirement or not. To ensure an appropriate level of protection, make certain that the hat carries a British Standard Institute (BSI) kitemark (or a similar national standard outside the UK). At the time of writing these are BS6473 for a riding hat, and BS4472 for a jockey skull cap. You will find these numbers inside the hat, but they are most easily recognised by their three- or four-point harness as opposed to the older, and less safe, two-point chin straps. During use, ensure that you do up the drawstring inside the hat if one is fitted, as this will provide a cushion of protection if you fall off and hit your head. You can expect to pay anything between £30 and £55 for a suitable riding hat.

In the USA the highway code varies from state to state, as do the legal requirements concerning the wearing of hard hats. The American Horse Shows Association (AHSA) recommends that all riders wear only headgear that meets or surpasses the ASTM/SEI (American Society for Testing Materials and /Safety Equipment Institute) standard. The AHSA

Don't forget to budget for your own riding wear when you are working out the costs that will be involved in owning your own horse. When riding regularly – every day, as opposed to only once every week or so – your jodhpurs, boots and raincoat will wear out far more quickly. Rainproof or leather full or half chaps are a fairly costly but warm and useful extra for day-to-day exercising, and they will prolong the life of your jodhs indefinitely. For shows and competitions you will need to budget for a smart outfit, too: a tweed or black jacket; a tie and/or stock plus stock pin; tidy leather boots – your scuffed and stained exercising pair will *not* do; and tidy accessories (whip, gloves, velvet hat cover)

also requires all juniors (under eighteen) to wear safety helmets in competition, and recommends that adults do as well. For safety, your daily riding wear should consist of:

■ A BSI standard hat that has never received a significant blow. If it has, it must be replaced.

■ A back protector if you intend to do any jumping.

■ A pair of riding gloves, either string or leather, in order to prevent chafing from the reins and to provide extra grip when the reins are wet from rain or the horse's sweat – though note that leather gloves will slip on leather reins when wet. Gloves will also help to keep your hands warm in the winter which will ensure that you can grip the reins sufficiently well to stay in control. Glove prices vary according to materials and quality, and can range from £1.50 to £20.

■ Riding boots. Whether long or short, these should have a suitable heel to prevent your foot from slipping through the stirrup, and a reinforced toe cap to prevent your toes from being crushed if the horse stands on them. Jodhpur boots may cost in the region of £30, while long rubber boots may cost around £40. Long leather boots will cost very much more, but they are not essential unless competing regularly to a high standard. A most comfortable arrangement for casual riding or jumping is jodhpur boots and leather gaiters.

■ Comfortable clothes, including jodhpurs and a suitable jacket, jumper or shirt for the time of year, are necessary for safety. Remember that your arms and legs should always be covered in order to offer some protection in the event of a fall, or against low branches. When considering the purchase of clothes, do not forget yard wear. There are now some excellent groom's overalls on the market, which are lightweight, comfortable and warm. These are a wise choice for protecting other, more expensive clothing.

■ You will also have to allow for show gear in your budget if you intend to compete. This will vary a great deal depending upon the type of competition, but you can often pick up some excellent bargains if you look around; this is one area where used clothing is a real money-saver. Most children grow so quickly that they hardly have any wear from their show clothes before outgrowing them, and because the initial outlay for new clothes is so expensive, people tend to look after them. Ask friends, or other horse club members, and you may be surprised to find that show clothes need not cost as much as you feared. However, do remember to look after them, and keep the chain going by passing them on when you have finished with them.

For your own safety it might be advisable to wear a back protector if you intend to do any jumping; most can be bought with shoulder pads as an optional extra

Farriery

Most horses in work will need shoeing every five to eight weeks, and even if your horse is not shod, it will still require regular hoof trimming. The old saying 'no foot, no horse' is very true, so it pays to ensure that your horse's feet receive expert attention. However, good farriers are hard to come by, most having far more horses and ponies to attend to than ideally they would like. The best way to get yourself on the books of a good farrier is by personal recommendation from an experienced horse owner. It will also help if you can arrange to have your horse shod along with others at your own premises, your livery yard or at a neighbouring yard.

You should try to avoid farriers who are always advertising in the local papers. While a newly qualified farrier may need to advertise, if he is good he will soon have his books filled and then advertising will cease. Ask your friends about the farrier they have – do their horses often lose shoes? Do they ever go lame after being shod? Do they play up when shod? Does the farrier always turn up within a reasonable time, or at least notify them if he will be late? Is he preparedto help them if a horse needs specialist or remedial shoeing? If you are not happy with the answers you receive, it may be wise to look elsewhere.

If you have not got a personal recommendation, you can obtain a list of registered farriers from your national farriers' association which, in the UK, is the Farriers' Registration Council PO Box 49, East of England Showground, Peterborough, Cambridge, PE2 6GU. A full set of shoes will cost between £25 and £35 (1996), while trimming will cost around £5 per hoof. Additionally, most farriers charge mileage, so be aware that this will increase the bill.

In the USA you should contact the American Farriers Association based in Lexington, Kentucky, an organisation which operates different certification levels and which would be able to recommend a certified local farrier. However, USA farriers do not have to be licensed; most people seek local advice from their vet or another professional when moving into a new area.

WORKING OWNERS

There is no question that owning a horse is a huge commitment and not something to be taken lightly. If you are still young, and it is your parents who are allowing you to have a horse or pony, you will give this little thought. But what if you have a family of your own and work commitments – can you care for a horse too? The answer is yes, but understandably, many people have doubts when buying a horse for the first time if they already lead quite a full life, with other responsibilities. Nonetheless, the number of working people who are buying a horse for the first time is increasing. There seem to be many reasons for this. For some it wasn't a practical thing to do in their teenage years and early twenties while they were trying to build a career or raise a family, and either time or finances wouldn't stretch. For others it seems the question of horse ownership never arose until they suddenly decided they wanted to own a horse, rather than ride someone else's. Whatever the reason, you may feel that owning a horse and working don't mix. However, it is possible if you want it enough.

ASSESSING YOURSELF AS AN OWNER

What sort of owner will you make? This is probably one of the hardest questions to answer in regard to ownership, especially as you must be honest with yourself. In order to help you to make up your mind, we will categorise what is really important, and what is less so. You should enjoy every minute with your horse, but unfortunately there are occasions when things go wrong. If you find yourself in such a situation, the last thing you should do is to shut yourself off and try to work it out alone; things will only get worse. There are lots of people out there who would be willing to help, so never be afraid to ask for advice. Riding clubs and the Pony Club are an excellent place to start; you will also meet many new friends and be able to take part in a whole variety of events and social functions. Owning a horse is fun, and buying one for the first time is special – but it is only the start of what should be many enjoyable years.

FINAL CHECKLIST

While owning a horse is a great thrill, don't forget that it is a constant learning process. Whether you are still a novice or are competing regularly, it is sensible to remember the importance of continuing with professional instruction. Bad habits tend to slip in unnoticed, and unless they are corrected while still developing, can be very difficult to eradicate. Similarly, having acquired a new horse, do not be too quick to ignore good advice. There are plenty of pitfalls that you can avoid if you are prepared to listen.

ESSENTIAL

- **Funds** – enough to feed and care for your horse without risk to its health.
- **Time** – enough to care for your horse's daily needs.
- **Dedication** – the desire to care for your horse before yourself.
- **Knowledge** – enough to care for your horse's daily needs without risk to it or yourself.

DESIRABLE

- **Funds** – enough to do the things you want to do with your horse, such as competing.
- **Time** – enough to have lessons and progress in your riding.
- **Enthusiasm** – to learn more about your horse and horses in general.
- **Skill** – in order to school and compete with your horse if applicable.

NON-ESSENTIAL

- **Funds** – for luxury items.
- **Expert knowledge** – as long as you know the basics, you can learn as you go along, provided you are willing to listen.
- **A horsy background** – you can become just as good an owner as someone who has grown up around horses if you persevere.
- **A house with stables and land** – but there are alternatives, a good livery yard being one.

Having satisfied yourself that you can cover all the essentials and maybe even some of the 'desirables', you should examine your own knowledge and ability closely, as these will have some bearing on the type of horse you buy.

With regard to knowledge, it is essential that you know how to:

- provide a horse with the correct food in the required amounts for its size, bodyweight, temperament and workload;
- carry out correct first-aid procedures;
- tack up or put on harness correctly, depending on whether the horse is ridden or driven.

COMMON PITFALLS TO AVOID

- **Buying the wrong horse** – so as to avoid costly mistakes always learn as much as possible about a horse before committing yourself to its purchase; but remember – the perfect horse does not exist.

- **Cash-flow crisis** – before buying a horse always consider all the costs involved, not just the initial purchase fee.
- **Ill health or unhappiness** – endeavour to satisfy all your horse's physical and psychological needs in order to ensure its well-being.
- **Being taken for a ride** – make sure you know just what the livery yard has undertaken to do for your horse and the exact costs involved.
- **Costly purchases** – only buy what you really need, and to ensure you are getting good quality, go to a reputable saddler.
- **Unnecessary accidents** – ensure that you wear a hard hat at all times when riding, and think before you act in all that you do with your horse – an unnecessary injury could cost you dearly.
- **No foot, no horse** – correct farriery is essential.
- **Getting into a rut** – always take lessons from an experienced instructor who caters for your particular interests.
- **Annoying others** – always be courteous to others, especially when on the roads and around the stable yard. Manners cost nothing, and a happy yard is a really enjoyable place to be.
- **Losing interest** – make sure you include plenty of variety in your riding, including lots of activities with friends.

Plodding round the same block on your own day after day is bound to become boring. So vary your route when hacking as much as you can – find out where the bridleways are, and use them; join up with friends – the horses usually like the company, too!; do a little jumping, go to the village show, join the local riding club: plenty of varied activity and there will never be _any_ chance of your losing interest!

PERFECT PROVIDER

Judy Holt had been riding at her local riding school for four years. At the age of eighteen, she had secured a fairly good job as a bank clerk which meant she would have enough money to buy her own horse. She enquired at her local livery yard and she was told they did have two vacancies for half-livery at £55 per week. This seemed to be within Judy's price range, so she set about finding the right horse. She looked in the classified advertisements of a well known equestrian magazine and marked those horses which she thought looked promising. Having ridden for four years she no longer considered herself a novice, and as she had jumped quite a bit on Dusty (her favourite riding school horse) she looked for a horse that would be a good jumper. The third horse she telephoned really took her fancy. It was described as a bay Warmblood mare of 16.1hh. The horse was five years old, but 'quiet as a lamb and sure to jump out of Grade C quite quickly,' said the owner. This horse seemed ideal, so Judy went to try her.

On arrival at the yard, Judy introduced herself to the owner and told her this would be her first horse, although she was an experienced rider. Upon seeing the horse, she immediately fell in love with its sleek head and jaunty trot. The mare behaved very well in the school and Judy said she would have her subject to a veterinary examination. Judy telephoned a local vet from the owner's yard, who agreed to come out the following day, so Judy laid a deposit of £300 (the asking price was £3,000). As Judy was at work during the day, she said she would telephone the vet when she got home, but firstly he asked her what she wanted the horse for and what standard of rider she was. She informed him that she was an experienced rider and that she wanted the horse for showjumping.

When Judy called the vet the following evening he told her that the horse had a few lumps and bumps, but nothing to prevent her from being a show-jumper. He said the horse appeared to be a nice mare, but that she was not a novice ride. This did not matter as Judy knew she could handle her, so she paid the balance and took possession of the mare, Tilly.

On Tilly's arrival at the livery yard, Judy suddenly realised that she would have to buy a saddle and bridle, not to mention all the other accessories such as a grooming kit and feed bins. However, she did have some savings and could just about afford to kit Tilly out with some good gear.

At first everything went well. Judy hacked out with some of the other riders and Tilly behaved very well. Then one day she decided to take Tilly out alone. She found out the mare was very nappy and would not leave the yard at all on her own. Judy gave her a smack with the crop, but Tilly started to buck and Judy ended up on the floor in a heap. She was a little shaken and bruised, but otherwise seemed unhurt. Nobody else had seen the incident, so Judy turned Tilly out and decided to wait until she could hack out with the others again. Everything was fine until Judy wanted to ride on her own again. She hoped that the past incident had been a one-off, but on attempting to leave the yard Tilly stopped dead and reared up. Judy became frightened and just froze while Tilly started to whirl around. Tilly did not seem to care what she was doing and scraped past the gate hook, cutting her side badly. She panicked and started to buck, throwing Judy high into the air. Sandy, the yard manager, was watching and she quickly took charge of the situation. Judy appeared concussed, and Tilly was bleeding badly from a large, gaping wound in her side. Sandy called an ambulance and her veterinary surgeon. Judy was taken to hospital where concussion was diagnosed and Tilly had to have thirty-eight stitches in her side, plus a course of antibiotics.

Once she came home from hospital Sandy told Judy that Tilly was not the right sort of horse for her, and that the mare should be sold on to someone more experienced. However, she would need to be schooled to eradicate her habit of napping if she were to fetch the £3,000 that Judy had paid. This schooling would cost £30 a week on top of the livery fees. Judy agreed, as although she would not admit it, she knew that Tilly now frightened her. Two weeks later the vet's bill arrived and Judy did not have the money in the bank to cover it. Then Tilly needed shoeing and worming, and the costs just seemed to mount up. Judy had to get a loan from the bank where she worked to pay it all off. Tilly was sorted out, and has now been sold to a competent teenager who is competing successfully with her. Judy now has no horse but is still paying off the monthly loan. She has given up the idea of owning a horse again.

MORAL *If you are going to buy a horse make sure you have allowed for all the costs before going ahead. This includes not only everyday expenses such as livery and feed, and capital expenses such as saddlery and the horse itself, but also unforeseen expenses such as vet's fees. Also, make sure the horse is right for you – take someone knowledgeable with you who can offer an expert opinion. Riding once a week at a riding school does not make you an experienced rider, so before you embark upon ownership try to ride and handle as many different horses and ponies as you can.*

3
BUYING A
HORSE

WHERE TO BUY

Having decided that you are definitely going to buy a horse, and after satisfying yourself (and perhaps your bank manager!) that you can afford to provide for it, the next stage is to start looking for one in earnest.

The most satisfactory way of buying a horse is by word of mouth. A personal recommendation from a friend or instructor about a horse or pony for sale can save a lot of searching and disappointments. If looking for a first horse you can try asking the secretary of your local riding club, and similarly, if looking for a pony for your child, the District Commissioner of your local Pony Club branch may know of a suitable one being sold. Many of the best ponies pass through the Pony Club in this way, so take the time to ask around before you move on to other buying methods. Unfortunately, however, the 'network' system of acquiring a horse or pony means that there are never enough 'recommended' ones to go round. Owners who have a really good horse are often loath to part with it, and even if they do decide to do so, it will probably be to someone who is well known to them.

Other ways of buying a horse are through auctions, a dealer, or advertisements in the local or equestrian press. The drawback to these methods is that you will know very little about the horse before you see it, other than what you read in the catalogue or what the seller or dealer tells you. In addition you will have very little time in which to make a decision unless the seller is prepared to agree to a trial period, which in all honesty is fairly unlikely.

BUYING FROM A PRIVATE SELLER

When buying an unknown horse you will have to make a decision on what you are told and can see about the horse in a relatively short space of time. To a certain degree you are therefore in the hands of the seller, and you have no way of knowing whether or not he or she is genuine. Unfortunately, you may not experience any problems with a horse until you get it home, by which time you may find yourself in a tricky and totally unsatisfactory situation; so beware. As a potential purchaser, you first need to have a clear view of what it is that you want. You then need to get yourself organised and ensure that you take all reasonable precautions during viewing and make all the necessary negotiations prior to purchase.

Private sellers usually advertise their horse for sale through the press, so this is the place to look when wanting to buy. You might also find cards posted in tack shops and feed merchants, so keep your eyes open wherever you go. The first thing to do prior to making any inquiries is to organise yourself. Buy a folder and write 'Horses for Sale' on it. This might seem a little silly, but I cannot remember the number of times in the past that I have scribbled descriptions on the edge of a newspaper or the back of an envelope, only to find that it disappears within seconds, usually as someone else's fire-lighter. If you follow these simple guidelines, you will always have to hand all the information that you require.

- Compile a list of all the things you need your horse to be, using three headings: *essential; desirable; totally unacceptable*.
- Study the advertisements, comparing your list to any that seem suitable. Remember that what is left out often says more about a horse than what is put in, so try to read between the lines and don't allow yourself to be persuaded by any cleverly worded descriptions.
- Mark any horses that appear suitable and transfer the information to a writing pad, using a separate page for each horse and putting the seller's telephone number at the top of each description. This will prevent any confusion when telephoning many advertisements in one day.
- Take a look at the information given about any horse you intend to enquire about, and then make a list of any omissions in the advertisements, so that you can ask the appropriate questions over the telephone before deciding to visit the horse.

(right) Compile a list of all the things you need your horse to be and stick to your intentions. For instance, if you want an established dressage horse, make sure the horse has competed regularly at the standard required; don't be swayed by cleverly worded advertisements that say the horse 'has a lot of potential' or 'will go far in the right hands'

(left) A pony such as this, that will do anything asked of it and look after its rider however unorganised or insecure he or she may be, is worth its weight in gold. If you are offered such a pony, or learn that it is available through a reliable friend, at least go and try it before you turn it down: better to buy the right pony six months too soon, because it is bound to take some finding when you *do* need it! Many of the best ponies pass through the Pony Club, which has an excellent word-of-mouth network to find the right pony for the individual child

READING BETWEEN THE LINES

As an example, let us consider the following two advertisements in relation to a fairly confident, first-time buyer of 5ft 6in (1.6m) who weighs 147lb (67kg). She wishes to own a good all-round type of horse with which she can have fun at local riding club shows.

Both horses seem to be worth considering, but let's take a closer look at each advertisement before we ring up.

15.2hh TB x Welsh

Bay gelding, 11 yo.
Good to shoe, box and in traffic.
Ideal schoolmaster, sensible in all respects.
A real gentleman. £1,500
Tel: 1987 654321

16hh TB x Irish Draught,

Grey mare, 5 yo. Good temperament,
100% clip, box and shoe.
Will go far in the right hands. £2,250
Tel: 1234 567891

HORSE 1 is a good size for our buyer and TB/Irish is a fairly popular cross. So far so good. A grey mare – well, the colour is fine, but our buyer would have preferred a gelding. Nevertheless, she decides that if the horse is suitable in all other respects perhaps its sex is not such a handicap. A good temperament indicates that it is amenable and should be easy to handle. That the horse is 100 per cent to clip, box and shoe is there for all to see.

OK, so where's the catch? In this case, you should have immediately been alerted to the fact that in the list of '100% to ...' there was no mention of 'to catch' or 'in traffic' and these are fairly standard things to mention if the horse has such qualities; so this is something you will need to ask the seller outright on the telephone.

Also take a look at the closing shot: 'Will go far in the right hands'. Immediately you should have thought, 'Why are the present owner's hands not the right ones?' This phrase is often used to indicate potential ability, but our buyer wants a horse with which she can compete confidently from the start. In addition the horse is just five years old, so one assumes that she still has quite a bit of learning and maturing to do herself. It looks as though our buyer should cross this one off her list. A good horse in prospect, but not right for her.

HORSE 2 is also an acceptable size, and slightly more 'common blood' suggests a more laid-back temperament. One advantage is that the horse is a gelding, which is what our buyer really wanted. Also, as he is eleven years old, he has seen a bit more of life and should be totally set in his ways, so if he isn't a good horse now, then he never will be.

He's good to shoe, box and in traffic which is all good news, but no mention of catching or clipping, so these are questions to ask over the telephone. 'Ideal schoolmaster, sensible in all respects and a real gentleman' indicate that this horse rarely puts a foot wrong.

This seems to be a real contender, but alarm bells start to ring when you look at the price: £1,500 is quite cheap for this horse, so you need to find out why he is being offered for this amount. This does not mean to say you would put the question in such a blunt form, because to ask outright could work against you.

Tact is needed in order to elicit the information you require. 'Why are you selling him?' may be a good opener on the subject. Also try and find out why the asking price is apparently so low: does he have any vices? Does he have a health problem? Ask, and if your questions are evaded, ask again until you get a straight answer. It may be that the horse has a blemish and the seller feels this will make him less attractive to potential purchasers (see page 41). However, armed with the facts you might decide that this would not affect your purchase decision so the horse would be worth looking at, and if found suitable in all other respects, could be a good buy.

QUESTIONS WHICH YOU MUST ASK THE SELLER AT THE OUTSET

1 How much are you asking? – It is pointless to run through the ensuing questions if the horse's price is clearly out of your league.

2 How old is the horse?

3 Why is it for sale?

4 How long have you owned it and how many owners has it had throughout its life?

5 Are you a horse dealer or a private seller?

6 What has the horse done, for how long, and how extensively has it competed (if appropriate)?

If the horse is good to catch this is usually mentioned in the advertisement. If it is not, remember to ask the seller over the telephone if it was simply missed out; a horse that is unwilling to be caught is usually to be avoided

7 Does it have any breeding history and/or papers?

8 Does it have good manners, and is it generally calm when being handled?

9 Does it have any stable vices, such as crib-biting, wind-sucking, weaving, wood-chewing, rug-tearing, door-banging or box-walking?

Ask what tack the horse is normally ridden in and why. The type of bit and bridle, and whether or not the horse wears a martingale, will provide important clues about what it is like to ride. If it is wearing boots and/or bandages, ask why: is this the owner's standard practice, or does the horse brush or knock into itself badly?

10 Does it have any ridden vices, such as bucking, rearing, napping or bolting?

11 Has it ever been known to bite or kick?

12 Is it good in traffic, safe when ridden in company or alone, and will it go first or last?

13 Is it easy to catch, clip and shoe, and good to box and unload?

14 What bit and tack is it ridden in?

15 Does it live in or out?

How to proceed

1 Having shortlisted a few horses, telephone the first seller for further details. Make sure you ask all the questions you want to and that you get satisfactory answers, even if they are not what you wanted to hear.

2 Don't try to convince yourself that things can be overlooked if they were marked down as either 'essential' or 'totally unacceptable' on your list. Write down all the answers you get under the telephone number you have just called, and add the seller's name and address. Cut out the advertisement and attach it to the details you have just written down, making a note of the date and where the advertisement appeared.

3 If you are satisfied that the horse is worth looking at, make arrangements to see it and jot down the time and place on your list. Place this list in your folder.

4 Call your adviser and ask if he/she will accompany you, as he will be able to offer valuable advice and check any claims the seller will make.

5 Even if you feel that you have the necessary knowledge to buy a horse alone, it is still advisable to take someone with you as a witness to all that is said.

6 On arrival at the place where the horse is kept, introduce yourself and give the horse an in-hand assessment (see pages 56–7). Inform the seller as to what you want it for and gauge his/her reaction, not just by what he says but by body language also. If he tells you a horse never refuses while avoiding your eye, twitching his hands and shuffling his feet, this suggests that he has certainly known it to refuse and is keeping his fingers crossed that it won't today.

7 If you like what you see, proceed to a ridden trial (see pages 60–1); but if you realise at this stage that this is not the horse for you, say so. Be polite and thank the seller for his/her time but do not prolong what is obviously an unsatisfactory viewing. You should not feel embarrassed to say 'no' to any horse, and must not allow the seller to persuade you against your own better judgement or that of your adviser.

When you arrive at the yard, ask if you can see the horse loose in its stable: you can go some way to assessing its character by observing its initial reaction to your presence. Does it look calm and friendly? Does it march over boldly and give you a shove in a rather aggressive manner? Or does it ignore you and look sulky?

If you like what you see so far, ask to see the horse ridden. It is important that you see how it behaves and moves with another rider before you or your adviser tries it

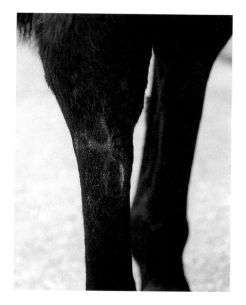

A blemished horse might be offered at a cheaper price and may prove a good buy if you don't intend to show it; but be quite sure that the superficial scarring you can see is *all* that is wrong with it, and that it isn't something which will cause problems in the future, such as lameness or arthritis

8 If you intend to proceed to a ridden trial, ensure that either the seller, or his/her assistant, rides the horse first. Providing you continue to like what you see, ask your adviser to ride the horse, and then do so yourself. (See also pages 60–1.)

9 Request to see the horse loose in its stable and watch it being tacked up. Also ask to see it loose in the field after exercise later on.

10 Together with your adviser, examine the horse's condition. (See also pages 56–7.)

11 Try to form an initial impression of suitability, but also remember that you may have arranged to see other horses. If you truly like the horse and have a feeling that it is the one for you, let the seller know of your keen interest and proceed to make arrangements for a veterinary examination. At this stage the seller may request a deposit, or you may want to give one in order to secure the horse. However, if you are not totally sure that this is exactly the horse you want, then do not pay anything. Tell the seller you will be in touch and that you wish to

give the matter some thought before deciding to buy.

12 If you do decide to lay a deposit, it is not unreasonable for the seller to expect 10 per cent of the asking price, and he will probably want cash, so be prepared for this. Always get a written receipt for any money you have parted with, and make sure the conditions of the deposit are clear; for example, that the deposit is subject to the horse passing a veterinary examination, or that you are allowed to try the horse further, say over a cross-country course if this is the purpose you intend for it. In the event that neither of these things happen, you are then entitled to a refund of your deposit.

13 When arranging a veterinary examination, try to have your own vet carry it out, or at least an independent one. Do not be fooled by the seller telling you that the horse passed a vet only a few days ago. If so, why didn't it sell, and where is the certificate to prove this claim? Do not agree for the seller to arrange the vet him- or herself.

14 Before you leave the yard, ask if you may have the horse on a trial period. Many sellers will not agree to this, fearing the condition in which the

horse might be returned if found unsuitable. A refusal does not, therefore, mean that there is something wrong with the horse, but simply that too many so-called 'buyers' prove to be without conscience.

15 After satisfying yourself on all accounts that this is the horse you wish to buy, inform the seller, and ask them how they would like payment. Most prefer cash or a banker's draft, or to have clearance on your cheque before the horse leaves their yard. Before you hand over your money, ask for a receipt and also a written warranty from the seller, detailing specific points that you have queried and received satisfactory answers to; for example, that the horse is free from vice, good in traffic, or has never bred a foal before.

16 Before leaving the yard, whether with the horse or if it is to be collected or delivered in a few days, make sure you get your receipt and warranty. The seller telling you that he will have it ready on collection, or will forward it in the post, is not good enough. Once home, put the receipt and warranty into your folder. Discard any papers that do not relate to the horse you have just bought, and put its name and date of purchase on the cover.

Be sure to see the horse jumped, if that is what you want it to do with you; and don't be fobbed off with the seller's assurances that it never *normally* refuses, but it may be a little tired because it went to a show yesterday. If he looks uneasy as he says this, you can probably guess that the horse is a less-than-keen jumper, and that he has prepared this excuse should it decide to dig its toes in today!

SUGGESTED CONTRACT OF SALE

I: Mr Seller

of: Sell it Horse Sales, Bankit Road, Happytown.

Have this: 15th day of June 199?

received from: Mr Unsuspecting, of Worry Lane, Broketown.

the sum of: £5,000

For the: Four Year Old, Grey Gelding

Named: Fortunate

I confirm that I have transferred ownership of this horse to

___*Mr Unsuspecting*___   and warrant that this horse: _____*Has no*_____

_____*stable or ridden vices and is good in traffic, to clip, shoe, catch*_____

_____*and box, and that he is fit for quiet riding and dressage.*_____

Should this horse be found not to comply with the above warranty, and there is written proof of this, signed by a qualified veterinary surgeon, stating in what respect the horse does not comply, I agree for the horse to be returned to me at the above address not later than:

_____*7 days*_____   from the date of this contract.

In the event of a dispute arising as to the compliance with this warranty, the horse shall be referred to a qualified, but independent veterinary surgeon who shall be nominated by: _____*Mr Notinvolved.*_____ The decision of this veterinary surgeon shall be final and binding on both parties.

As witness the hands of the

parties have this _____*15th*_____ day of _____*June*_____ 199_*?*_

Signed: _____*Mr Seller (the seller)*_____

In the presence of: _____*Mr Witness*_____

Occupation & Address: _____*Loss Adjuster, Guilty House,*_____

_____*Court Lane, Fairshire.*_____

Signed: _____*Mr Unsuspecting (the buyer)*_____

In the presence of: _____*Mrs Witness*_____

Occupation & Address: _____*Book Keeper, Guilty House,*_____

_____*Court Lane, Fairshire.*_____

BUYING FROM A DEALER

If you mention to many people that you are thinking about buying from a horse dealer, they might try and persuade you do otherwise. Dealers have a bad reputation as being shady characters who like nothing better than to 'rip you off', or at best, to off-load their bad horses onto unsuspecting new owners who don't know any better. However, this attitude is changing, and in the main this is because dealers are quite a decent lot who simply want to earn a living doing what they love best – being with horses. Of course, you will always get the odd one or two who will still try it on, but no more so than the average private seller. In fact, if you buy from a dealer you will receive additional protection in law. Providing you inform the dealer what you want a horse for, and list any faults or conditions that are unacceptable to you, if he/she subsequently sells you a horse that exhibits one or other of these unacceptable traits, you can claim against him/her. Similarly, if you tell the dealer that you want a showjumper and, after purchase, the horse refuses at every fence, you would have cause for redress and could make a claim against him/her. However, the dealer is also protected in that if he or she advised you that the horse was not suitable for jumping and you bought it anyway because you liked it and thought it would do the job you wanted, you would have no redress.

As you can see, the dealer/buyer partnership is one built on trust, and many customers return time and again when they are looking to buy another horse, or sell the old one. Most dealers will try to match your needs with any potential horse, and if the horse proves unsatisfactory they will usually aim to exchange it for one that is more suitable. Remember, dealers have a reputation to uphold, and without dedicated, repeat buyers, their businesses would not last long. Word of mouth is a very powerful selling tool, and a bad reputation could take years to throw off, if at all.

BUYING FROM AN AUCTION

Buying from an auction can be a very satisfying experience. But it can also be horrendous for the unprepared. As with horse dealers, horse auctions have had rather a rough time of it, and while in the past they had a reputation for getting as much money as they could for a horse without any consideration given to the buyer, today this is largely an unfair criticism. Small sales in local villages may still prove unsatisfactory places at which to buy a horse, but the larger auction houses now provide an excellent service. One advantage, of course, is that you can see many horses at one time, and you can also take the horse away with you the same day. You may also be able to buy a suitable horse more cheaply through an auction than in a private sale, so, all things considered, there is a lot to recommend it.

Mr Terry Court, FSVA, ARVA, FAAV, of Russell, Baldwin & Bright Auctioneers in the UK, offers these few words of advice:

Always remember that *bona fide* firms of auctioneers have a reputation to uphold, and that they are there to help both seller and purchaser; the auctioneer should be looked upon in the same light as your veterinary surgeon – a professional who is doing a professional's job. As auctioneers we

The larger auction houses provide an excellent, professional service nowadays, with horses worth a great deal of money passing through their hands

find there are no disadvantages in buying horses at auction sales – well, at least the ones organised by us. We believe that it is only right to offer both first-time and regular buyers a first-class service, with the strictest of conditions of sale that are monitored annually, together with an advisory service which is second to none.

Russell, Baldwin & Bright Auctioneers has embarked on a British Standards policy and will hopefully be registered under ISO9002, thus making sure that all their services are of a standard which is acceptable to the international community. Such assurances offer peace of mind, so before you go to buy a horse at auction, do consider the quality of service and conditions offered by the auctioneers.

We believe that our auctions are ideal for first-time buyers, as purchasers do have very much more protection from our conditions of sale than they would if buying privately. All our sales are conducted under the strictest conditions of sale, to protect both seller and purchaser, and at all sales there are veterinary surgeons available to act on behalf of purchasers, and agents are available for advice.

When considering a sales venue, enquire about trial facilities. Is there

Smaller local markets often provide a convenient outlet for people anxious to off-load their problem horses, so beware! Animals are offered with no guarantee as to temperament, ability or reliability at these sales, and there is generally little comeback for the buyer

somewhere flat where you can see the horses trotted up? Is there an exercise area where you can see the horse being ridden? If jumping horses are for sale, are there adequate facilities for jumping?

Also ensure that all horses entered are accompanied by an entry form completed and signed by the owner. This constitutes a formal contract between seller, auctioneer and purchaser under the strict conditions of sale.

BUYING IN THE USA

In the USA people wishing to buy a horse will usually go to a professional trainer for assistance. They will then maintain a relationship with this trainer for ongoing help with the horse. There is certainly more scepticism in the USA than in the UK about buying horses, and the general feeling about buying is 'buyer beware!'. In the barn-type of stabling in the USA, it is normal for horses to be presented for inspection on crossties in the aisle, which makes it difficult to know what stable vices they might have. The doping of horses is also thought to be more of a problem than in the UK, and yet potential buyers don't seem particularly 'wised up' to the idea

of getting blood drawn at the time of vetting in case of any soundness or character changes at a later stage (see also pages 108-110). One advantage of buying a horse in the USA is that, unlike the UK, most sellers will happily offer a trial period provided the horse is going to a professional yard – they will not, however, if it is going somewhere unknown.

In the USA there are three main types of sale:

- bloodstock sales to cater for the TB market;
- sport horse sales, although there are few of these as they haven't caught on yet in the same way as in the UK;

- livestock auctions. These are very basic, and a wide range of horses and ponies are put through the ring. Unlike the UK, there is seldom a catalogue or any printed information about the horses – you just buy what you see before you. Horses stand in stalls and are just brought out to show to people and possibly walked and trotted up. A horse will only be ridden just before it is sold in the sale ring, so there is little time to evaluate a potential ridden purchase. There is a livestock market of this sort in most regions, run under an annual licence which costs around $15.

A GUIDE TO FIRST-TIME BUYERS AT AUCTION SALES

DOS

- Before attending the sale, make sure that you have decided in your own mind exactly what type of horse or pony you need to buy to fit your requirements. At no time be persuaded to alter those requirements at a later stage.

- Contact the firm of auctioneers to make arrangements with them for you to be able to purchase. If you are not going to pay by cash, make sure that banking arrangements with their bankers have been cleared.

- Only buy from horse sales where there are properly printed catalogues.

- Have the auctioneers send you a catalogue in plenty of time for you to study it. If the seller makes it available, try to inspect your prospective purchase at the seller's home before it leaves for the sale.

- Make sure you have studied the 'conditions of sale' printed in the catalogue, and make sure that, as a prospective purchaser, you will have every redress if the horse or pony is not as described.

- Make sure you have redress to a veterinary surgeon's advice following the sale.

- On your arrival at the sale site, introduce yourself to the auctioneers and, if they have advisory agents, ask them for their advice and help.

- Make sure you have properly inspected those horses and ponies which you have marked as possible purchases.

- If after those inspections you are not totally happy with the lots you have marked, do not try to find an alternative.

- If you find a lot to be satisfactory to your requirements, decide either by yourself or with the help of the auctioneer's advisory staff the amount of money which you think might justifiably be paid for the animal.

- Position yourself in the sale ring so that you may be seen easily by the auctioneer.

- As soon as the appropriate lot comes into the ring and you have to bid, make sure that you make your bids distinctly. (It is usually also possible to phone in and leave an 'offer' if you cannot attend the sale. The auction company will then contact you later if you have been successful.)

- After the sale has been concluded and if you are a successful purchaser,

If you intend to bid, position yourself in the sale ring so that auctioneer can see you easily

make sure that you carry out the instructions as per the 'conditions of sale'. If any faults in the description of the animal are spotted, either by you or the vet in his examination, inform the auctioneers who will take up your case against the seller.

DON'TS

- Don't attend sales that are not catalogued (although in the USA you have little choice).

- Don't attend sales which are not run by *bona fide* companies of auctioneers.

- Don't buy out of catalogues where the vendors' names are not stated.

- Don't bid if you have not inspected the horse or pony previously.

- Don't bid if you don't understand the 'conditions of sale', and make sure that these have been made clear to you by the auctioneers.

- Don't be palmed off with statements such as 'There's no need to bother the vet with that particular animal as I can assure you that the problem/worry/ blemish is of no consequence'. Always make sure you receive professional advice about any problem you are concerned about.

- Never pay more than you can afford.

- Never go to an auction unless you have made proper arrangements, and have organised haulage and so on beforehand.

- Never buy and take your purchase home without having it checked, even if you feel that everything is all right.

JARGON BUSTING

When you study advertisements and catalogues you will see a whole range of abbreviations which are necessary due to the constraints of space. However, don't let all this faze you; it is not a secret code, merely another necessary part of buying or selling a horse. Here are some of the most common abbreviations in use, followed by some of the expressions used in the trade that are often designed to impress the less experienced and of which you should be more wary.

AHSA	American Horse Show Association
N/H	National Hunt
BHD	British Horse Database
NTR	National Thoroughbred Register
BHS	British Horse Society
O	open
BSJA	British Show Jumping Association
ODE	one day event
BSPS	British Show Pony Society
PB	part-bred
FR	first ridden
PBA	part-bred Arab
Han	Hanoverian
PBW	part-bred Welsh
HIS	National Light Horse Breeding Society (formerly Hunters' Improvement Society)
PC	Pony Club
PN	pre-novice
HOYS	Horse of the Year Show
PUK	Ponies Association (UK)
HT	hunter trials
RC	Riding Club
h/wt	heavyweight or (HW)
R/D	ride and drive
I	Intermediate
RIHS	Royal International Horse Show
ID	Irish Draught
SHP	show hunter pony
LDR	long distance ride
SJ	show jumping
LHC	life height certificate
TB	Thoroughbred
LR	lead rein
WH	working hunter
l/wt	lightweight (or LW)
WHP	working hunter pony
MM	mountain and moorland
WPBR	Wetherby's Part-Bred Register
m/wt	middleweight (or MW)
XC	cross-country (or CC)
N	novice
YO	years old

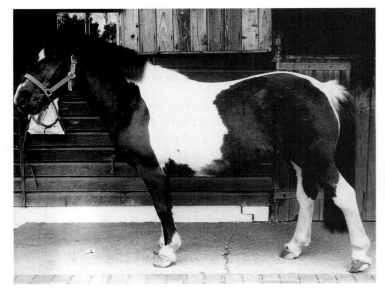

You might ask yourself if this pony is merely a 'good doer', or one which might very readily become obese, with all the problems that come with it

A huge jump over a big spread: such a horse may genuinely be described as 'scopey'

EXPRESSION	MEANING	BEWARE OF
Aged	A horse over eight years of age.	A horse without any proof of age being sold as much younger than it really is (get your vet's opinion).
A good doer	A horse that always looks in good condition on just grass, or on a minimum amount of food for work done.	A horse wth a propensity to obesity.
A 'green' horse	A horse that is still inexperienced, either due to its young age or lack of training.	A disobedient or problem horse being passes off as simply 'green'.
A good 'pop' in it	A horse that has the ability to jump high fences.	A horse that 'cat leaps' over its fences, often unseating its rider.
Loves to jump	A horse that thoroughly enjoys jumping.	A horse that on first sight of a fence charges at it and is unstoppable.
Never stops	A horse that never refuses when jumping.	A reckless horse that jumps fences even if completely wrong for take-off.
Scopey	A skilful horse that can easily jump large or difficult fences.	A horse that jumps very high, even over small fences. If you are inexperienced it may jump you out of the saddle.
Not a novice ride	A horse that is only suitable for an experienced rider, because it is very keen or excitable.	A horse that constantly misbehaves, or has an established ridden vice such as rearing.
A fun ride	An enthusiastic, lively horse, that is still obedient.	A horse that jog-trots or one with whom you have to be constantly on your guard for fear of it playing up.
Schoolmaster	A horse that has done it all and seen it all, that is virtually 'unflappable' – a good confidence-giver for the novice rider.	A horse that will teach you everything providing you let it have things all its own way!
Would suit novice/nervous rider	A quiet, easy-to-handle/ride horse which does not easily become upset.	A horse that is so stubborn or lazy that it will not do more than a steady walk.
For sale through no fault of its own	A horse that is for sale purely because of its owner's changed circumstances. The owner may have lost his/her job, for example.	A horse that has got the better of its owner, until the owner is convinced that he or she is useless.
Seen to (name of vice: **windsuck**, for example) occasionally	A horse that infrequently displays the abnormal behaviour associated with the named vice.	A horse that happily continues this vice while its owner is at work all day only to stop it when brought in and ridden

EXPRESSION	MEANING	BEWARE OF
Playful	A youngster that has yet to mature and needs to be taught obedience.	A horse that treats you like an enemy, biting and kicking you at every opportunity.
Great potential in ...	A horse that has all the makings of being an able jumper, or dressage horse, or good at any other sphere mentioned.	A horse that could do it if it wanted to, but has no intention of even trying.
Will make a ...	A horse that looks as if it could be an able competition horse, or has breeding which indicates such qualities.	A horse that with which someone else has tried and failed, only to sell it on as 'untrained'.
Up to weight	A horse that can carry the full weight of its category: about 168–182lb (76–83kg) for a l/wt, 182–196lb (83–89kg) for a m/wt and 196–224lb + (89–102kg+) for a h/wt.	A really cobby, common type of horse with short, fat legs and a body to match.
Good all-rounder	A horse that enjoys and is fairly good at all equestrian disciplines.	A horse that simply does not have the ability to do well in any discipline.
Bombproof	A horse that is excellent in traffic and go is never scared by loud noises or sudden movements.	A horse that won't move or have a at any equestrian activity.
Snaffle-mouthed	A horse that is well mannered and under control when ridden in a snaffle bit.	A horse that is fine in a snaffle while in the school, but needs something much stronger in other environments.
Easy to box/catch/shoe, etc	A horse that behaves as required during the mentioned activities.	Is not reliable in things that are *not* mentioned such as 'clip' or 'in traffic'.
Ideal first horse/pony	A very well mannered horse or pony that is quite willing to do exactly as required by its rider/handler.	A horse or pony that will do no more than a sedate walk.
Owner giving up	Where the horse's owner has to sell it due to a change in personal circumstances, rather than any fault of the horse.	An owner who is giving up because they can no longer sustain the broken bones and bruises inflicted upon him/her by the horse.
Forward-going	A horse that needs little provocation to move forward through the paces; generally keen to work as asked.	A horse that is so keen to be off that it neither stands still when being mounted nor stops when required.
Quiet to handle	A horse that is well mannered both in and out of the stable.	A horse that is well mannered in and out of the stable, until you ride it!
Extremely laid-back	A horse that remains totally calm and sensible however upsetting or exciting the circumstances.	A horse that almost impossible to get motivated because it is so bone idle and stodgy.

A horse that rears up and boxes at you is certainly *not* just 'being playful'. This stallion is probably just showing off his natural exuberance, but would you have the experience and the confidence to handle him?

A horse or pony that is quite competent at all the equestrian disciplines, and is happy and reliable in his work, is known as a 'good all-rounder'

The 'ideal first pony' must have impeccable manners, it must be utterly reliable in all respects, and above all it should be willing and happy to do exactly what it is asked by its young rider. In fact these qualities are just as much pre-requisites of the second pony, which will be required to look after its charge off the leading rein. Children graduate very quickly from the 'first pony', and soon want to gallop, jump, hunt and take part in showing classes on their own, as well as tack up, groom and look after their pony without Mum fussing around. Generally this presupposes an older pony, since such reliability is unusual – though not unknown – in a youngster; and such ponies are usually passsed on by word of mouth through the Pony Club network. So if this is what you are looking for, keep eyes and ears open, and don't be afraid to ask likely people

TRIALS

When you go to see a horse with a view to purchase, you are putting both the horse and its owner 'on trial'. How you assess the horse will depend upon:

- why you want it;
- what you intend to do with it.
- your own ability;
- your personal likes and dislikes.

Only you can tell whether it is ability, looks or temperament which carries the highest merit for your requirements, so assess the horse first on why you want it. If you want a good jumper, see it jumping before you assess its other qualities. Similarly if good conformation is of the utmost importance, study this immediately, *before* you look at the horse in action. It is so easy to be impressed by a horse's good qualities (and remember, the seller will always try to show these off as much as possible) that you can get carried away and buy the horse because it is such a brilliant jumper, when you really only wanted a well mannered hack; or because it has such a lovely temperament that you feel you can improve its paces for dressage. If the horse does not do as you want at the trial, do not buy it, no matter how much the seller assures you it is simply having an off day.

Assessing the potential purchase

When you are looking at a horse from the ground you should get an overall feeling of balance: the head should be in proportion to the neck, the neck to the back, the back to the quarters and so on. While it does take time to acquire 'an eye for a horse', you should be able to spot anything that is obviously out of place. If your eye is drawn to a particular feature it will be because it is either first class, or at fault.

Taking time to study different horses in the show ring and also doing a little 'ringside judging' will pay off when you go to view because in noting what a well put-together horse looks like, you will know instinctively when something is wrong even if you cannot say why. Of course, you will also have the opinion of your adviser, but knowing what is right and wrong will help you to feel happier about your selection.

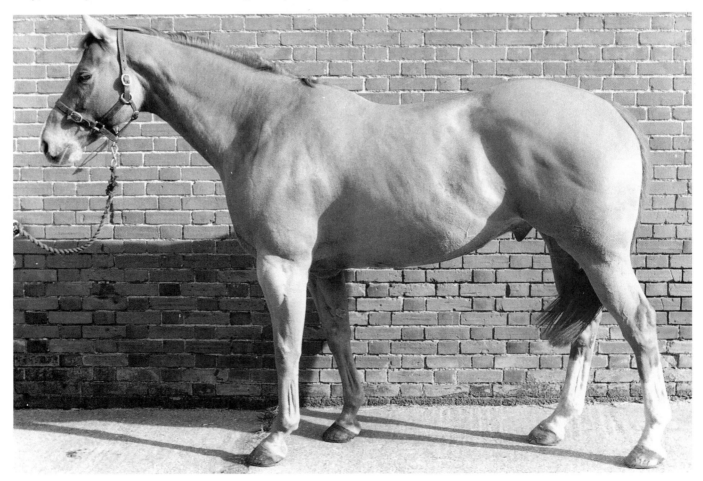

When assessing the horse in hand, look for an overall impression which is pleasing to the eye, the different parts of its body well balanced and in proportion to each other. If any one feature catches your attention then it is generally because it upsets the overall picture *ie* it is probably at fault. This horse is nicely proportioned

Conformation

The first thing to decide is how important the horse's conformation is to you. Horses come in all shapes and sizes, but generally, each individual's make and shape tend to govern its suitability for a given purpose. Show horses must have good conformation, and to a certain extent so must dressage horses if they are to look elegant and move well. Showjumpers and endurance horses, however, may come in all shapes and sizes and will still be perfectly capable of doing their job. When looking at any horse ask yourself (and your adviser): 'Is this horse suitable for the job required of it?' In order to judge this, follow these simple guidelines which, as well as helping you to assess a suitable horse, will also prevent you from passing over any that may not be super equine athletes, but may well be totally suitable for your purpose.

Study a horse's head before you look at any other part of his body because his head will tell you almost all you need to know of his character, his type and his attitude to life. Here you have one plain and one quality head, but both look kind, calm and well disposed. The quality head probably implies the better horse, but if you are looking for a weight-carrier, then the plain head will be the type *you* want!

- Unsoundness should be treated with suspicion.
- Bad conformation does not mean that the horse is unsound or is likely to become unsound, but certain faults could very well predispose the horse to health and/or soundness problems in the future.
- Pretty is as pretty does; good looks are no guarantee of ability.
- Always assess the horse's overall structure and appearance – you cannot assess individual parts in isolation from the rest of the body.
- Be aware of the horse's condition. A horse may look in good condition, but what's underneath?

As the perfect horse has yet to be born, and because everyone reading this book will have different requirements from the next person, it would serve little purpose to give a long description of 'good conformation'. (Should you require such details you can find them in the book *Showing Masterclass*, written by the author and published by David & Charles.) Instead look on pages 83–93 in Chapter 4, where you will find a list of conformational faults together with their possible effects and potential problems and, which I hope will prove far more useful in assessing your potential purchase for your chosen activity.

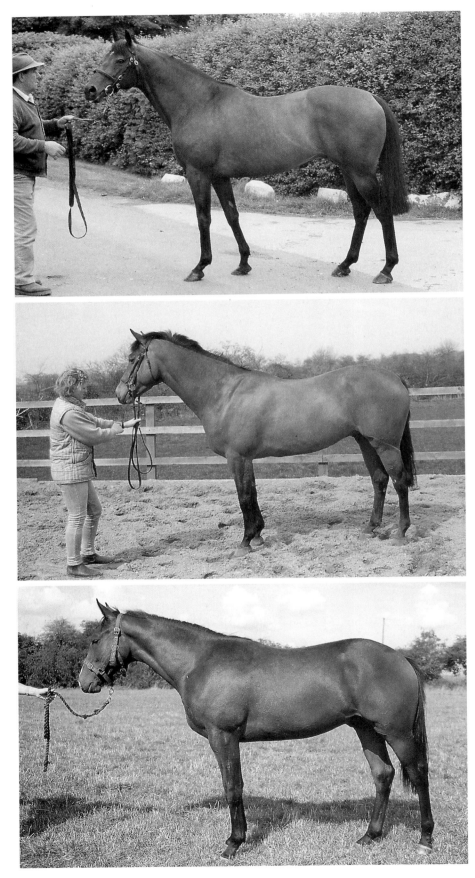

If you compare horses A and B, you will see that horse A is more comfortably put together than the one below it, horse B; he has a good slope to his shoulder (45° is the ideal) and a good length of neck; overall he has a good topline, his neck fits very well to his shoulder, his shoulder to his girth, which has a good depth, and he is strong over the loins which makes a good 'fit' to the quarters. He has a good angle to his hock – they are not too straight – and also to his pasterns. If you were looking for faults, his pasterns are rather too long, certainly in front, and his off-fore hoof looks flat: a flat, shallow sole is a fault often found in Thoroughbreds.

Horse B has a weak, hollow topline; his neck and head seem too big for the rest of him and his middle is rather slung between his front and back end; this means he does not have the same muscle and strength over the loins as can be seen in horses A and C. Compared to horse A he doesn't have such good length from the croup to the less powerful hindquarter. He is also straight in his hocks, which could well predispose him to such problems as curb, thoroughpin and spavin; look for these if you are considering a horse with hocks like this. He has upright pasterns, too: this tends to give a jarring ride, and could lead to problems such as ringbone and sidebone.

Horse C is not as good as horse A, but he is better than horse B because he has a stronger topline, a better angle to his hock, and overall he looks more comfortably proportioned. However he could have a little more slope to his shoulder, and a shade more length to his neck, and this makes him less good than horse A. But the conformation of his front-leg pastern is the best of three horses: less sloping than A, and not as upright as B.

So which would you prefer to take home?

Manners

Manners are extremely important in any horse. It is most unwise to disregard a horse's bad manners in view of even exceptional ability, and it is foolish to think you can reform an ill-tempered horse. It is simply not worth the effort, as such a horse will always prove tiresome and may also be a danger to you. Unless you are so experienced at the handling of horses that you can afford to ignore such advice, your first buying rule is: 'Be sure that the horse is well mannered both in and out of the stable'. So, how can you find out about this in such a short space of time? Well, first you just observe the horse in its stable, and then you carry on observing it while it is being handled and tacked up. Are its ears forward, unless listening to some-thing? Does it seem generally relaxed and happy? Are its eyes bright and relaxed? If you feel happy about this, ask if you may handle it, perhaps to tack it up or turn it out. Beware of a horse that lays its ears back at you or its owner; is fidgety and jumpy all the time; shows the whites of its eyes, snorts a lot and generally seems unsettled. Finally, take a few moments to think about the horse. Did it stand still when asked? Did it lead well? Did it stand still for mounting? Was there anything that seemed to bother it unduly?

Ability

Assuming that you are happy with the horse's manners, you will want to assess its ability according to your needs. Here the rule is: 'Be truthful about yourself'.

There is nothing wrong in wanting to see the extent of a horse's abilities; after all, if you progress it is as well to know your horse's limitations. However, don't tell the seller that you want the horse to jump Grade C tracks when really all you want is a horse capable of jumping at local riding club level. If you over-horse yourself you will end up paying more than you need to, and you may also find that you have bought a horse that is too much for you to cope with.

When assessing ability you must ensure that the horse is capable of all that you will want to do. If you want to do dressage, see the horse put through its paces and then ride it yourself to get the feel of it. Horses often do not 'ride' as they 'look to be going'. If you want to jump across country, then ensure you try the horse over a cross-country course. Showjumps will not do, and vice versa – a showjumper should not be tried over a cross-country course. If you need a horse that is good in traffic, try it out on the road. Do not leave anything to chance, and do not take the seller's

A display of blatant aggression. One of these stallions has broken away from its handler and is attacking the other, and even in an entire, such arrogant behaviour should not be tolerated: bad manners such as this are quite unacceptable, whatever the horse's other credentials

word for it, however genuine you feel he or she is. Make sure that if you buy the horse you will have only yourself to blame if it turns out to be unsuitable.

Character and temperament

Character and temperament are related to a horse's manners, yet the difference is that manners are taught, and usually a horse's character and temperament are those that it was born with. You can build on a horse's character and temperament, but you will not be able to change them to any degree, so be sure that you actually 'like' the horse as it is. Do you want a bit of sparkle, or would a more laid-back type be more suitable for you? Often a horse's temperament may reflect that of its owner, not because one

(right) While a horse or pony can be taught good manners, its character and temperament are irreversible: it can be used and abused until it turns sour and crochety, but if it was born with an amenable disposition, sensitive handling will make it amenable again. *You* will have to judge whether a horse is by nature grumpy, or really good-natured!

(above) As a buyer, be truthful about what you want. Do not, therefore, tell the seller you want to event at a high level if all you really want to do is jump around your local hunter trial course

feeds off the other, but simply because we tend to be drawn to horses that have traits similar to our own.

Health

Health is an important consideration and this is why the veterinary examination (see Chapter 5) is so important. Unless the horse is healthy it will not be able to carry out the work required of it, and it may end up costing you a fortune in veterinary fees. However, ill health does come in degrees and you may find that the horse has a problem with which you can cope and which will not affect your requirements of it. A condition such as chronic obstructive pulmonary disease will probably affect a competition horse that is stabled a great deal, but may be less likely to worry the horse that can live out and is only used for hacking. The important thing is to take your vet's advice. Talk over your needs with him, and if necessary discuss a possible plan of health care if this is realistic. Also consider the asking price carefully. Does it truly reflect the horse's condition and its resale value?

The veterinary examination is important because if the horse is not basically sound in limb and wind it may not be able to cope physically with the work you want it to do. If it is constantly lame or under the weather, it could end up costing you a fortune in vets' fees

Influence of the dam or sire

A horse's parents are of consideration in spheres such as breeding, showing and racing, but tend to be less important where it is ability that counts. Many top-class horses come from parents that had no form; similarly top-class parents have produced low-class horses. There really are no guarantees. The best advice here is that unless the pedigree is of absolute priority for breeding lines or similar, then simply judge the horse that is in front of you.

Of course, what breed the horse is will have some bearing on your decision. For instance, you will not want a Thoroughbred if you require a horse that will live out all winter with the minimum of care, nor will you want a Shire horse if you intend to compete in showjumping. However, having selected your preferred 'type' of horse, try to judge the horse on its own merits, not on what its sire or dam, brothers or sisters have accomplished. While such accomplishments may be of interest to you, and more so if there seems to be a pattern of ability in any given field, at the end of the day each horse is an individual and must be treated as such. The exception here is when buying a foal or youngster, when often you will have nothing else to go on other than the parentage or the achievements of relatives.

Pedigree and parentage may be important in breeding and racing, but sometimes a youngster may not seem to take after its parents at all. Atlantic River Dance, the filly shown above, is out of the TB Miss Frère, and is by Atlantic Dancer, a British Warmblood stallion (below). Compared to father, the filly is much longer in the cannon bone and altogether more rangy, and would appear to have taken after Mum (below left); she has inherited her father's rather short neck. Perhaps she will also inherit the Warmblood's generally steadier and less excitable temperament

Past history

Buying a horse with 'papers' does mean that you have a record of its parentage, and obviously, this is of value in the case of mares which are likely to be used for breeding. However, more important is the question of past history. When looking at a potential purchase, try to find out all that you can about the horse from as far back as you can. Ask the current owner, and try to find out the names and contact details of previous owners. Phone them up and ask them about any points, good or bad, that they can relate about the horse. They may shed some light on matters such as why the horse is bad to box, or why it has a scar on its leg. By building up a past profile, you can often learn a great deal about a horse's character, and such knowledge can go a long way when it comes to dealing with problems that may present themselves in the future.

EXAMINATION IN HAND

In order to assess all the preceding qualities, you should establish your own examination procedure, which will help to prevent you skipping over something that could prove to be very important. Follow this procedure at all trials and you will ensure that each horse gets the same inspection, thus preventing one horse from looking better than another unless it really is. Your inspection should include the following points:

■ On arrival at the yard, observe the horse in its natural environment, whether this is in the stable or out in the field. If it is tense or nervous, be wary, because on its own territory it should be relaxed.

■ Take note of how it is standing. Resting a hind foot in a relaxed pose is fine, but resting a forefoot or pointing a toe is a sign of trouble.

■ Take note of how it reacts to ordinary handling. How does it react when you walk in the door? Is it interested and inquisitive; does it put its ears forwards, or does it turn its backside to you with its ears flat back, making it quite clear that it does not intend to let you get any further? Talk quietly to it and give it a pat, then ask it to move over by pushing its side. If it responds well there is a good chance

Ask to see the horse stood up, and try to fix an initial impression of him in your mind

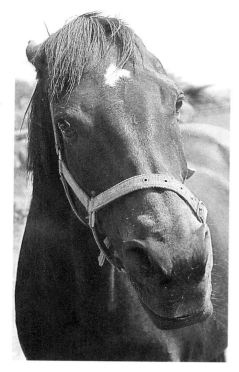

You will see immediately how the horse reacts when you approach: with his ears flat back and his nostrils curled back like this you can assume he is unfriendly – and probably grumpy by nature, not just made surly by inconsiderate treatment

that it has been taught good manners. However, if it tries to barge past you, it is either plain bad-mannered or uneducated. Either way, you will have to spend some time in teaching it what is required.

- Ask to see the horse stood up outside its box, or in the field on a flat surface.

- Study it 'overall' and fix an initial impression of it in your mind.

- Run your hands over its limbs, feeling for any abnormalities. If there are any, note them in your mind and then discuss them with your adviser or veterinary surgeon; but do remember that it is uncommon to find a horse in work that has totally clean legs, splints being the most common defect (see page 97).

- Lift up the horse's feet and study its

hooves, noting their shape and soundness.
- Study its frame individually from head to tail. Does its head look in proportion to its neck, its neck to its body, and so on?
- Stand behind it and ask to see it walked away from you and then towards you on a loose contact. You should look for a free and easy walk and a generous stride.
- Ask to see it trotted up on a loose lead-rein so that you can observe its natural movement.

Your first consideration is whether or not the horse is level. If not, proceed no further with the assessment as it would be foolish even to consider an unsound horse. Next, see whether it seems to move close or wide in front or behind, or whether it shows any other peculiarity of movement such as dishing or brushing.

How much of a margin you have for such defects depends upon their severity and what you want the horse for. A horse that dishes will never get anywhere in the show-ring, but it might be

'No foot, no horse', so after the head, pick up and inspect the feet. A good foot shape would be circular rather than oblong, the sides not too straight, with a well formed frog and fairly prominent heel. You could feel quite happy with this foot – though you might suggest it needs shoeing!

quite capable of jumping a Foxhunter class, for example. If in doubt, ask your vet's opinion. Remember, good movement means that a horse is more likely to stay sound for its working life, while a deviation from good movement will inevitably put strain on its limbs and joints.

- Tell the seller exactly what you want the horse for, and have him/her assure you verbally, in front of your adviser, that the horse is suitable for your purpose.

- Check the horse's age as far as possible (see page 58–9) and ask the seller its age as well . Also assess the horse's mouth to ensure that it is neither under- nor overshot, which can cause eating, and possibly bitting problems.

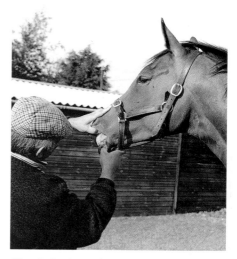

Check the horse's age as far as possible by examining his teeth, but also ask the seller to state his age in front of a witness

- Ask categorically whether the horse has any undesirable traits, and spell out exactly what you mean, even if they are things that would not in fact prevent you from buying the horse. Ask the seller: 'Does he weave?', 'Is he good in traffic?', and so on. A genuine seller will not mind what you ask, provided that you are civil and businesslike.

- Providing you are quite happy, you should proceed to a ridden trial.

HOW OLD IS YOUR POTENTIAL PURCHASE?

In the early twentieth century it was thought possible to age horses confidently by examining their teeth. Recent research has shown that the methods used are not as accurate as most books would indicate. When you buy a horse documentary proof of age is always much better than relying on an examination of the teeth.

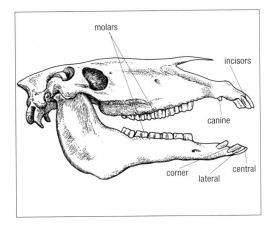

The first evidence we consider when ageing a horse is the number and type of teeth present (Fig 1).

The three temporary (or 'milk') incisor teeth on either side of the jaw have erupted by the time the horse reaches 9 months of age (Fig 2).

At around 2½ years old the first permanent incisor appears (Fig 3) (note that it is much larger and extends further up the gum than its temporary companions). The next two permanent incisor teeth erupt at 3½ (Fig 4) and 4½ years of age (Fig 5) respectively.

Male horses usually have canine teeth or tushes, although they may only be present in the lower jaw (Fig 7), and appear at around 4 or 5 years of age. Female horses do not usually have tushes at all.

Between 5 and 10 years old we age horses by examining the biting surface of the lower incisor teeth. At 6 years old there is a circular infundibulum or cup mark in the centre of all three incisors on each side (Fig 8).

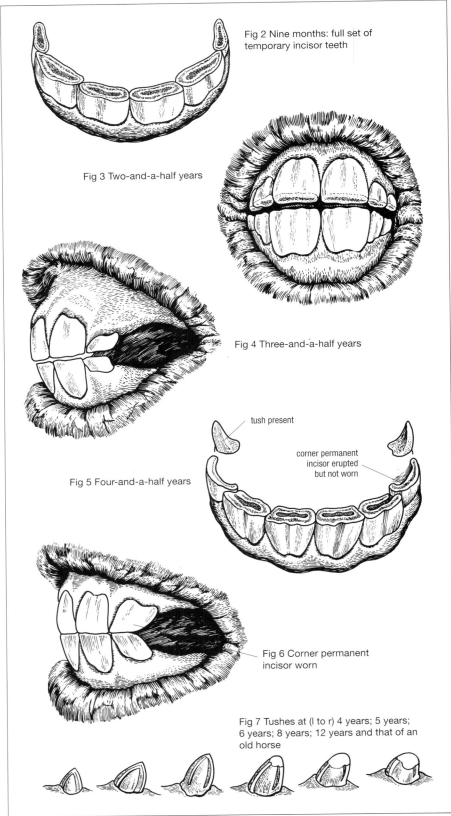

Fig 2 Nine months: full set of temporary incisor teeth

Fig 3 Two-and-a-half years

Fig 4 Three-and-a-half years

Fig 5 Four-and-a-half years

tush present

corner permanent incisor erupted but not worn

Fig 6 Corner permanent incisor worn

Fig 7 Tushes at (l to r) 4 years; 5 years; 6 years; 8 years; 12 years and that of an old horse

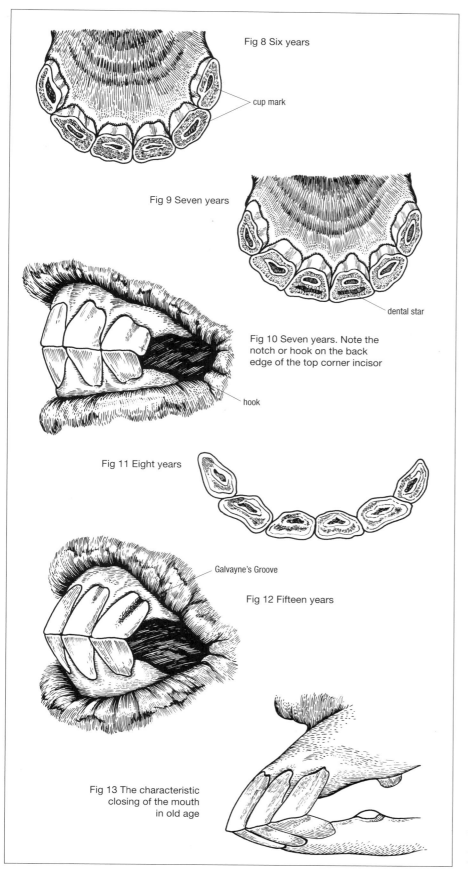

Fig 8 Six years

cup mark

Fig 9 Seven years

dental star

Fig 10 Seven years. Note the notch or hook on the back edge of the top corner incisor

hook

Fig 11 Eight years

Galvayne's Groove

Fig 12 Fifteen years

Fig 13 The characteristic closing of the mouth in old age

At 7 years old a dark mark, the dental star, appears in front of the cup in the central incisors (Fig 9). Because the upper and lower jaws do not meet exactly at this time, a hook develops on the rear edge of the upper lateral incisor (Fig 10). It disappears after a year or so as the teeth meet more precisely. Some horses develop a similar hook at around 11 to 13 years old, so it is important not to jump to any conclusions over age just based on the so-called '7-year hook'.

At 8 years old the dental star is present in the lateral and possibly the corner incisor (Fig 11). Horses older than 8 are referred to as aged, not because they are old physically but because there are no accurate means of estimating their age.

Some horses develop a dark groove down the side of the upper corner incisors. Mr Galvayne, who discovered this feature, felt it was an infallible way of ageing horses. In 1912 he claimed that he was never wrong in his estimate of a horse's age, but since he didn't work on horses whose age was precisely known it was difficult to contradict him. The groove first appears near the gum around 10 years of age. By 15 years old it extends halfway down the tooth (Fig 12). By around 20 years old it extends all the way down the tooth. By 25 years old it extends halfway down again, and by 30 years old it has disappeared. The length of the groove may vary on each side of the jaw, so both need to be examined.

It is important to remember that all these aids to ageing horses are averages. There may be a spread of several years between the time that one horse develops a particular feature and the time it appears in another horse. Poor environment and certain soil conditions increase wear on the teeth, with the result that the horse appears older than it really is. Even the eruption of the incisor teeth is subject to some variation.

It can also by useful to obtain a quick impression as to whether one is looking at an old horse or a young horse. With age the cross-section of the incisor teeth changes from round to triangular, and the angle at which the upper and lower incisors meet changes from almost vertical to acute (Fig 13).

RIDDEN EXAMINATION

Do not proceed to a ridden trial unless you have given the horse as good an examination from the ground as you are capable of, have seen it move, and are still of the opinion that this is a worthy prospect for your needs. Always ask to see the horse ridden before you undertake to ride it yourself. It is up to the seller to provide a rider. If he does not, then you should assume that there is a 'reason' for him not doing so. Seeing a horse ridden provides you with the opportunity of studying its movement and manners. It is far better to watch the seller being run away with or bucked off than for this to happen to you if the horse turns out to be less than co-operative! Providing a competent rider, if not riding the horse him- or herself, is in the seller's best interests as it should go well for someone used to riding it.

Be aware of the horse's general attitude. Is it willing and co-operative, or does it set itself against the rider? Does it stand still when being mounted? Ask to see it walked, trotted and cantered on both reins so that you can establish the quality of its gaits. Notice whether it is stiffer on one rein than the other. Unless you have indicated that you want the horse purely for dressage or ridden showing, ask to see it jumped, even if you have no desire to use it for jumping – remember that its resale value is important. Also ask to see the horse ridden in the open and out on the roads in traffic. Then ask your expert adviser to ride it.

Providing you still like what you see, it is time to confirm your impression of the horse by riding it yourself. Always ensure that you are fair to the horse and its owner. Do not get on the horse with your coat flapping in the wind, or let your children run around it or generally

Ask if you can see the horse ridden before you ride it yourself – if it is going to explode or be nappy, it is better that it's not with *you* on board! Then if you continue to like what you see, ride it yourself; hopefully the way it goes will confirm your initial favourable impressions

give it cause for concern. Before you mount, check the girth and stirrups, and once mounted, walk off calmly and allow yourself time to relax and get the feel of it. Move into trot on both reins when you feel ready, and then to canter. Do a few circles and transitions, and you will soon realise whether you like the feel of the horse or not. You may not be able to put it into words, but often you will know whether a horse is right or wrong for you. While you will want to see the extent of the horse's capabilities, do not expect to get on and have it going as well as when its usual rider rode it. Allow it time to relax before asking too much of it. It will take time to build a rapport, but you should at least get a feeling of suitability.

Lastly, providing all is still well, ask to take the horse onto the road. Going along with another rider is fine, but do make sure that it will also go alone. Have it lead as well as follow another horse on both the outward and the homeward journey, as some horses are nappy when going out and extremely keen to get back. On your return to the yard, hold the horse still outside the yard's entrance while your companion takes his/her horse into its stable. Ask your horse to walk away past the entrance and then back again. If it refuses, it is showing signs of nappiness and you should be wary of it.

By the time your feet hit the floor upon dismounting, you will know intuitively whether this is the horse for you. If you feel it is, you may want to lay your deposit there and then, to prevent anyone else from seeing the horse and making an instant decision to buy it. If so, do ensure that your deposit is subject to a veterinary examination (see Chapter 5). Alternatively, you may wish to give it some thought and perhaps return again for another final look. This way you do run the risk of someone else buying the horse before you, but you will also prevent yourself from making a costly 'spur-of-the-moment' decision.

First impressions

Your initial impression of the horse will undoubtedly be a lasting one, and in many cases will prove to be the one that counts. However, do be sure to give

Going along with another rider on the roads is fine, but do ensure that the horse is happy to go alone as well. Have someone follow you in a car if you are at all worried

each horse a fair trial and take in all that you can about every one. Always be alert and ask the questions that are on your mind. For instance, when the horse is being tacked up, ask if the bit that is being used is its normal one. If the horse is wearing a thick numnah (saddle pad), ask why. If there is no martingale, ask if the horse usually wears one. If the horse is not clipped in winter but is in work, ask why, and so on. Although some things will inevitably slip your mind, always try to cover anything that puzzles you. Do not be afraid to ask questions. If the seller is evasive and does not want to give you answers, then ask yourself another question – why?

The time will come when you know for sure that a particular horse you have looked at is the one for you, and then it is just a case of getting the vetting and financial formalities sorted out before you finally own a horse of your own.

BUYING BLUES

Janet Short had already owned three horses, so she considered herself to be fairly experienced. However, she was quite a nervous rider, and when she went to buy her fourth horse she informed the dealer of this fact. The horse she was interested in was advertised as a ten-year-old gelding, novice ride, with no vices; just the sort of horse Janet wanted. The dealer seemed a very fair man who was prepared personally to guarantee the horse's soundness, and said if the horse failed to please in any way he would swap him for another one without any fuss. Janet decided to buy the horse and as money was a little tight did not have him vetted, especially as the dealer was going to guarantee him.

When Janet got the horse home (which she had named Charlie) he did seem to be a perfect gentleman. However, over the course of a week she began to realise that he could be very bolshy and would whip round in the stable and threaten to kick. He also had an intense dislike of motorbikes and would literally gallop off down the road whenever he heard one.

Janet called the dealer, who said he was sorry to hear about her trouble, that he did not have anything else suitable at the present time, and that he would look for one for her. He did seem such a nice man, so Janet left it at that and waited, and waited – and waited. After seven weeks she called the dealer again, who said he had been looking but still had not found anything suitable. Janet asked whether he would take the horse back anyway and refund her money; he said he could not do that but would keep looking for her. Another six weeks went by and Janet heard nothing. She called the dealer again, and got the same story yet again. She began to realise that she had been well and truly 'taken for a ride'.

By this time Janet was totally fed up so decided to sell Charlie herself. She advertised him as a nice looking ten-year-old gelding. The first person to view him was not a good rider at all, so Janet said she thought the horse was unsuitable. However, a man called Peter, who could ride very well, then came to try the horse. He asked outright if the horse had any problems, and Janet, being honest, told him he could be grumpy in the stable and did not like motorbikes very much. Peter took Charlie out on the roads, and on their return seemed quite happy. He had not met any motorbikes, but he felt that as the horse was otherwise sensible he could handle him. He did not seem too bothered about Charlie's lack of stable manners as he felt sure he would teach him some. He then tried to haggle over the price, offering Janet £500 less than she was asking. She decided to cut her losses and agreed to sell. Peter said he did not need the horse to be vetted, so the following week he paid his money and took the horse. Janet was sorry to see him go, but decided to take her time looking for another horse, especially as she had to boost her depleted funds first.

Eight months later Janet got a call from Peter threatening to sue her, as Charlie had been vetted for sale and it turned out he was fifteen years of age, not ten. It also appeared that he had chronic obstructive pulmonary disease (COPD). Janet was thrown into panic. It had never occurred to her that Charlie was older than the original dealer had told her, and she had never seen or heard him show any evidence of COPD, which she knew would have meant he would have been coughing, or had a discharge from his nose. Extremely worried, she called a solicitor.

The solicitor informed her that any misrepresentation on her part was innocent, in that she had relied upon the description given by the original dealer. He asked her whether, at the time of purchase, the dealer gave her any cause to doubt him. Janet said he had seemed quite honest and had agreed to exchange the horse if he turned out to be unsuitable. She then explained what had followed, and asked the solicitor whether Peter should have had the horse vetted. His advice was that Peter could say the same thing to her. If she had had the horse vetted in the first place, his true age would have been revealed, and any health condition would have been discovered had it been present at the time. Obviously the horse could have developed the condition while in Peter's ownership and this seemed likely as Janet had not seen any evidence of it.

The solicitor advised her that if the case came to court she should defend herself through innocent misrepresentation. It was also likely to help Janet's case that Peter had waited eight months before complaining.

Janet put all these details down in writing and sent them to Peter. She had no response, but a few weeks later she heard that he had managed to sell Charlie on. The new owners had not had the horse vetted either.

MORAL *Always have a horse vetted before purchase, and ensure that you try him under all the conditions that you will be exposing him to once you have bought him. Also, always study the horse in the stable to ensure he is well mannered, or at least so that you are aware of any faults.*

4
THE UNDESIRABLE HORSE

ONE MAN'S TRASH IS ANOTHER MAN'S TREASURE

There is no such thing as a perfect horse, so when looking to buy you must try to find one that strays least from your ideal. In theory this sounds quite easy – you simply look at a number of horses and choose the one with the least number of faults. However, it is not that easy at all. Say you want a horse that jumps well, has no blemishes and no stable vices. The first horse you see jumps like a stag, has perfectly clean limbs, but weaves for 24 hours a day. The second horse has no stable vices, jumps well, but has a splint on each front leg, a curb and a bone spavin. Horse number three has nice clean limbs and no stable vices, but refuses to jump half a metre (two feet); and so it goes on. In reality, you simply have to decide what your absolute priorities are and be guided a little by your gut reactions. You will certainly have to make a slight compromise, but when the right horse comes along you will invariably know.

Buying a horse is such an individual thing that it is impossible to say what constitutes a good or a bad one. What is right for you may be totally wrong for another person and while you might be unable to accept certain failings, they may be the exact qualities that are of the utmost importance to someone else. While one person couldn't care less about a horse's temperament provided it jumped clear consistently whenever at a show, another would rather it knocked every pole down as long as it was a lamb when handled. As the requirements of all those reading this book will be vastly diverse, what follows is a look at the most common faults and vices which frequently dissuade people from buying horses. What you must do is decide from the reasons given whether the problems are worth living with if the horse seems suitable in all other respects. Even if it seems to have more than one fault, these may be insignificant to you and so it may still prove to be suitable. However, you must always bear in mind that you may wish to sell the horse on at some stage, and the more problems it has, the lower the asking price should be.

VICES AND BAD HABITS

BAD IN TRAFFIC

What is it?
A horse that misbehaves in a number of ways when it sees or is passed by vehicles.

How will it affect the horse/me?
It will put the horse, you and other road users at risk from accidents.

How can I tell?
Ask to see the horse ridden in traffic. If all seems well, try the horse yourself, both in company and on its own. Some horses are fine with cars but spook when approached by large, rattling lorries or tractors.

Is this the horse for me?
Yes, if you live in a quiet area where there is little roadwork, or are an experienced rider who is prepared to retrain an older horse, or to educate it if it is still young and 'green'. Even so, think carefully if the horse is seriously traffic-shy, because even the quietest village will probably have the daily milk tanker or school bus passing through, and more probably a lot of agricultural traffic and you can't guarantee never to meet them.

BAD TO BOX

What is it?
An aversion to travelling. The horse refuses to go into a horsebox or trailer.

How will it affect the horse/me?
The horse will become anxious or stroppy when you attempt to load it.

How can I tell?
Only by asking the owner outright and insisting on seeing the horse loaded in your presence. Some horses prefer a box to a trailer, or vice versa.

Is this the horse for me?
Only if you do not intend to travel or are prepared to spend some time in re-educating the horse to convince it that being in the box is not so bad after all.

Establish the nature and degree of the problem, too: perhaps the horse will go into a trailer without a partition, but not with the partition in place, or even swung over; perhaps it needs a companion – Red Rum had a sheep, and wouldn't load without it! Perhaps it will go in a lorry, but not a trailer. Find out the exact nature of the problem, *then* decide if you can cope with it, particularly if otherwise the horse is right for you.

BAD TO CATCH

What is it?
A horse that runs off when you go near it in the field.

How will it affect the horse/me?
It will have a very annoyed owner.

How can I tell?
Ask for the horse to be left out in the field until your arrival. Then ask if you may catch the horse yourself, with the owner in attendance.

Is this the horse for me?
This can be a very annoying and time-consuming habit. There are solutions, however, so if the horse is right for you in all other respects, then this behaviour might be worth trying to overcome, but you will need a great deal of patience; solutions often involve long-term retraining and persuading the horse that being caught is acceptable to it. Such retraining is also extremely time-consuming, so this problem will almost certainly be unacceptable if you work full time and have to fit in your riding before you leave at 8am, or if you are fully committed to raising a family and have to fit the time you spend with your horse into a busy daily programme.

BAD TO CLIP

What is it?
A horse that is either frightened or bolshy when clipped.

How will it affect horse/me?
The horse may become very anxious at the sound of clippers and its behaviour will alter. It may be dangerous, simply refuse to stand still or sweat up so much that you cannot clip it without sedating it first which is expensive and a nuisance.

How can I tell?
Only by asking the owner outright and insisting on seeing how the horse reacts when clippers are near it. Just because it is clipped when you view it, do not take this as a sign that it is good to clip. For all you know, it may have had to have been sedated.

Is this the horse for me?
Yes, if you are competent at handling horses and using various methods of restraint, or are prepared to employ a professional to do the job for you.

Besides, sedating a horse in order to clip it is really a perfectly viable solution nowadays. Although quite expensive because the vet must administer the drug, this is probably the best and easiest solution with a difficult horse: it remains standing, is sufficiently co-ordi-

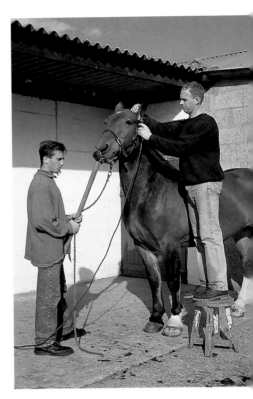

nated to be moved around a bit, but remains completely relaxed, cool and calm. The drug wears off after about 1¼ hours and the horse just 'wakes up' calmly. So don't be put off by this problem if otherwise the horse is what you want.

BAD TO LUNGE

What is it?
When a horse has either not been taught to lunge properly, or not at all.

How will it affect the horse/me?
It won't unless you had hoped to lunge it as part of its exercise or work schedule.

How can I tell? Ask to see the horse lunged while viewing.

Is this the horse for me?
Yes, if lungeing is not important, and in many cases a horse that is bad to lunge is only a reflection on the person who attempted to train it; in most cases the horse can be improved, if not totally re-educated. Anyway, and there are alternative forms of exercise. Having said that, it is always useful if a horse *will* lunge 'properly' because it is a valuable form of exercise and a way of keeping it in work should bad weather or minor injury or unforeseen circumstances prevent it being ridden. If you have not lunged a horse before, enlist the help of a knowledgeable friend. If you really like the horse, being bad to lunge should not constitute a reason to turn it down.

BAD TO SHOE

What is it?
The horse misbehaves during shoeing or trimming.

How will it affect the horse/me?
The horse will need re-educating with the help of your farrier.

How can I tell?
Only by asking the owner outright, insisting on seeing the horse shod, or by talking to the horse's farrier, if you can find out who this is. You can simply slip into the conversation a question like: 'Who shoes him – Joe Bloggs?' Which might just get a response like: 'Oh no, we have Fred Smith.' In which case you can phone Fred Smith and ask him about the horse, or get your own farrier to do this if he knows Fred Smith.

Is this the horse for me?
Talk it over with your farrier before purchase. Is he willing to help re-educate the horse? If it is seriously troublesome, then it may not be worth the risk to your farrier.

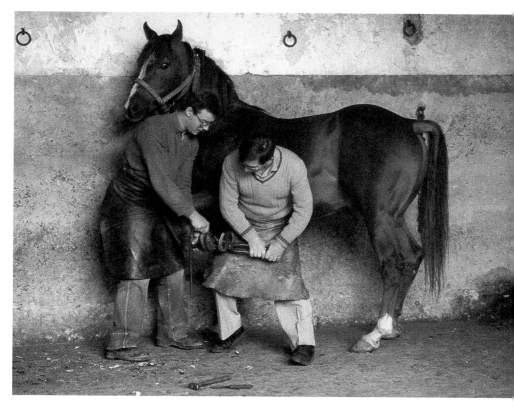

BARGING

What is it?
When the horse pushes into and past you in order to get in or out of its stable.

How will it affect the horse/me?
You may get squashed or trampled.

How can I tell?
By seeing the horse handled and by handling it yourself. See if it pulls you along without any respect.

Is this the horse for me?
Only if you are strong enough to control it while teaching it good manners. This horse or pony is not suitable for a child.

BITING

What is it?
When a horse either 'nips' or openly bites people or other horses.

How will it affect the horse/me?
It will affect you, and any other horses kept with yours, as you may all get bitten.

How can I tell?
The horse will attempt to bite you or its handler, or others in the field (other than in play). Observe the horse in various settings. Does it only do it when it is being tacked up, or is it always trying to bite?

Is this the horse for me?
Not if you are a novice owner or a child. The best way to keep a biter is to muzzle it. There are other forms of prevention, but think very carefully before buying.

BOLSHINESS

What is it?
A total lack of respect for handler or rider.

How will it affect the horse/me?
You may get hurt if you are not strong and quick.

How can I tell?
By seeing someone handle and ride the horse and by doing so yourself.

Is this the horse for me?
Only if you are not at all frightened of the horse and have enough knowledge, patience, understanding and confidence to handle and also to re-educate it.

BOLTING

What is it?

A horse that runs off with its rider.

How will it affect the horse/me?

The horse will endanger its own life, your life and the life of anyone else who gets in the way.

How can I tell?

You can't unless the horse does it when you ride it or unless you can talk to previous owners or people who know the horse. Try to find out as much as possible.

Is this the horse for me?

No. A horse that bolts is a real danger to anyone, however experienced. (Bolting is not the same thing as being difficult to stop.) Even so, try and find out if it bolts for a particular reason: perhaps it panics at rattling lorries or barking dogs, or when it is over-excited; then decide if the circumstances in which you will ride it will preempt the problem. Thus if your riding is largely in an arena or manège – dressage or showjumping – it may still be a horse which will suit you.

BOX-WALKING

What is it?

This is when the horse continually walks a circle around its box.

How will it affect the horse/me?

The horse may fail to put on weight and may exhaust itself if the habit is extreme.

How can I tell?

Look at the bed, is there a track in it? Observe the horse for a good while, preferably unnoticed by it.

Is this the horse for me?

Yes, if you intend to keep the horse out for much of the time, although such a horse is also more likely to fence-walk. You might consider that its ability makes it worth putting up with the problem. Even so, if the habit is confirmed it will make its general management difficult: it will walk its weight off, the tendons and joints of its legs will be subjected to unnecessary wear and tear, it may wear out shoes very quickly, and it will ruin any bedding within minutes. Can you be bothered with such aggravation?

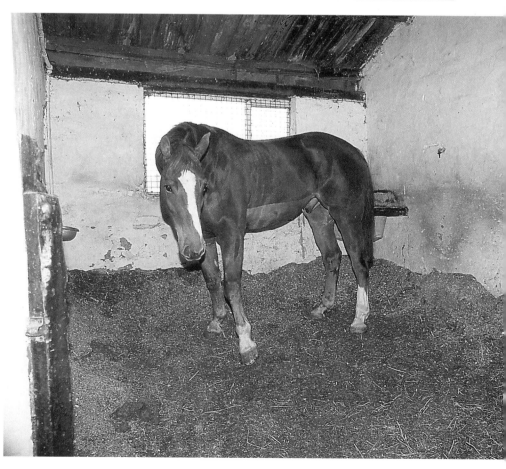

BUCKING

What is it?

When a horse kicks up its back legs when ridden.

How will it affect the horse/me?

It may simply be a sign of overexuberance.

How can I tell?

By watching the horse being ridden. Try to establish whether the buck is a playful, excited buck or a real bronco-type buck designed to get the rider off.

Is this the horse for me?

Not if you are a novice or nervous rider and the horse regularly gives real bronco-type bucks. Strict schooling will be needed: do you have the knowledge and experience? If so, then the horse is worth considering, particularly if it is a youngster which has simply been allowed to get away with it.

CRIB-BITING

What is it?

As windsucking (p82), except that the horse has to grab hold of an object in order to do it.

How will it affect the horse/me?

As windsucking.

How can I tell?

As windsucking.

Is this the horse for me?

Crib-biting is not as bad as windsucking in that it can often be prevented for most, if not all, of the time. In the stable you simply have to ensure that there is nothing the horse can grab hold of, so board all the walls flat, put a metal strip over the door and remove all fixed mangers and equipment. In the field, run a strip of electric fencing around the fence line. Put on a cribbing collar which prevents the horse arching its neck in the way characteristic of this habit. Consider whether it would be practical to implement these measures, then decide if the horse is really worth the hassle. Sometimes the habit is resolved by a change in management – the horse is turned out more, allowed the freedom of a yard rather than being shut in a stable, given more stimulating work.

DIFFICULT TO TIE UP

What is it?
A horse that pulls back or rears when tied up.

How will it affect the horse/me?
The horse may injure itself when pulling away or rearing.

How can I tell?
By seeing it tied up.

Is this the horse for me?
Only if you are quick-witted, have sufficient knowledge and are prepared to re-educate it – though it may in fact be less of a problem than it appears. Some horses are quite happy to be tied up in a trailer, or while you are busy doing things with them – shoeing, clipping, mucking out – but just don't like being left alone tied up. And some will only pull back so far, but panic if they are brought up short by a short rope; if you pass a longer rope or lunge line through the tie-up ring, then attach a block or ring on the end, they will run back but not be stopped short, and will stop themselves. So establish the degree of the problem, then decide if you can cope with it.

DOOR-BANGING

What is it?
The horse bangs the stable door with its front hooves or knees; some horses only do it at feeding times, others whenever they feel like it.

How will it affect the horse/me?
The horse may damage its knees.

How can I tell?
By looking at the horse's knees and observing it for some time, unnoticed by it.

Is this the horse for me?
Yes, if it will be living out for most of the time, and if it will respect a breast-bar in the stable. There are other methods of prevention but they are not always successful.

DOOR-OPENING

What is it?
The horse learns to open its stable door with its teeth.

How will it affect the horse/me?
The horse will escape from the stable if preventive measures are not taken.

How can I tell?
Watch to see if the horse plays with the catch or the door fittings.

Is this the horse for me?
Yes, there are special safety bolts which will thwart this habit. You will just have to remember to take a clip with you if the horse stays in a different stable, at a competition for example!

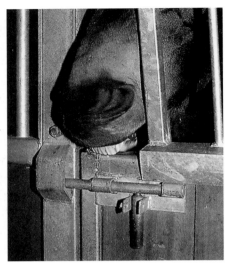

FIELD-BULLYING

What is it?
The horse bullies other horses when in the field.

How will it affect the horse/me?
It won't, it will affect any other horses in the field, unless yours comes up against one tougher than itself, when there may be a fight. However, it will make you both unpopular with other owners.

How can I tell?
By observing the horse in the field. Ask to see it out with other horses before purchase if this is the environment you will be keeping it in.

Is this the horse for me?
Only if you are keeping it stabled for most of the time and/or turned out on its own. You might be able to find a companion that this horse takes to, but a field-bully is a real nuisance and can never be cured. It will be particularly distressing if you have to keep it at liery, when its behaviour will incur the wrath of other owners.

HEADSHAKING

What is it?
When a horse continually shakes its head when ridden or out in the field.

How will it affect the horse/me?
The horse may become irritated and lose concentration, thus affecting its ability. You will never do well in dressage competitions.

How can I tell?
By observing the horse when ridden, or out in the field.

Is this the horse for me?
It all depends on what you want the horse for and why it does it. Many horses do it in reaction to little midges biting them, in which case you can put a hood on. Take advice from your veterinary surgeon about a clinical cause before putting it down to psychological disorder. It can be a very annoying habit when hacking out or working the horse outdoors, so don't buy it unless you know the cause and are confident of a cure or that effective management will be a solution. It would be quite unacceptable if you want the horse for competition, with the exception of perhaps long distance riding: dressage judges would penalise it very heavily, and it would compromise any jumping ability by upsetting the horse's balance and therefore accuracy.

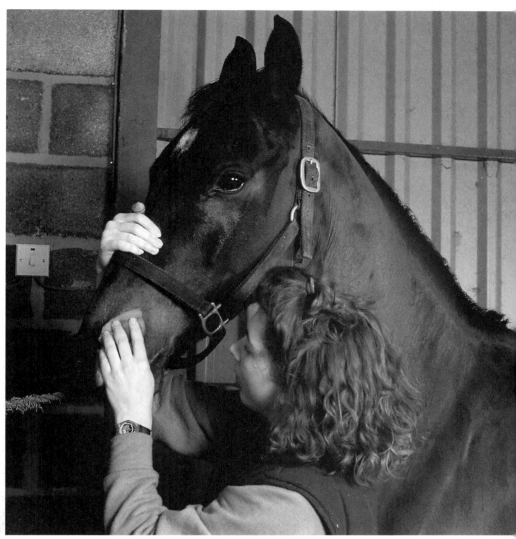

HEADSHY

What is it?
The horse does not like you touching, brushing or putting tack on its head.

How will it affect the horse/me?
It may bash its head on the wall in order to get away from you.

How can I tell?
It will show if you attempt to handle the head and try to put on the bridle.

Is this the horse for me?
With patience you may be able to improve the horse considerably, but you will need to earn its trust. Check that there isn't a physical reason: a cut on the ear or poll, or badly fitting tack, or rough handling by the current owner, any of which you can resolve easily. Even so, a novice or a child might find this behaviour worrying, so consider whether this is the right horse.

JOGGING

What is it?
The horse will not walk but continually jogs along when ridden.

How will it affect the horse/me?
The horse may sweat profusely and lose weight when ridden regularly. You may also find that you get an aching back and shoulders.

How can I tell?
By seeing the horse ridden, and by riding it yourself out on a hack, both alone and in company.

Is this the horse for me?
Not if you are a novice or nervous rider. A jogger can be retrained by an experienced rider. It is usually a sign of excessive energy, or that the horse has never been made to walk and trot properly when required.

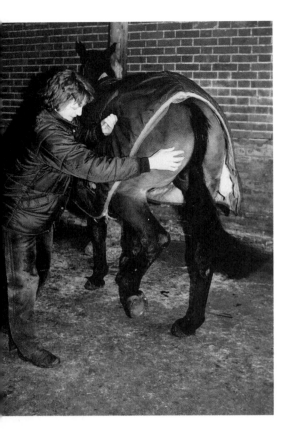

KICKING

What is it?
A horse that attempts to, or actually does, kick at its handler or other horses.

How will it affect the horse/me?
As with biting.

How can I tell?
As with biting.

Is this the horse for me?
Kicking is often worse than biting because you cannot muzzle a horse's leg! Do not buy a confirmed kicker unless you are experienced and simply want the horse for its ability and are prepared therefore to manage it.

LAZINESS

What is it?
This is when a horse is reluctant, or even refuses to work.

How will it affect the horse/me?
The horse may put on weight and its rider may lose weight!

How can I tell?
By seeing the horse ridden and by riding it yourself.

Is this the horse for me?
It depends upon the reason. Is the horse lazy because it is overweight, because it has stuffy conformation, or simply because it has a lazy disposition? You may find such a horse an asset for a totally nervous rider who needs to be led, but he/she will soon outgrow such a horse once his/her riding progresses. Consider whether you might be able to improve on the laziness and are also prepared to put in the necessary work to do so, or whether you would always be fighting a losing battle. It may also be lazy because it isn't feeling well, so consider its physical condition: does it look thin? wormy? overworked? out of condition? A good worming and a sensible diet for a month or two may revolutionise its desire to go forwards. So if it is lazy, but looks ribby and lack-lustre, give it a second look because this may not be its true disposition. A young horsem, too may just be lacking in muscle and co-ordination; another year and he is bound to be stronger and more motivated.

MANE/TAIL RUBBER

What is it?
The horse rubs its mane and tail, often due to a condition such as sweet itch.

How will it affect the horse/me?
The horse will become bald in these areas, and may even create sores on its crest and dock.

How can I tell?
Inspect the hair. Is it thin and wispy? Are there signs of rubbing on the neck? If the horse only rubs in the summer and you are buying in the winter there is little you can do other than obtain a warranty on this point from the seller.

Is this the horse for me?
This is a tiresome habit, though it it is possible for it to be alleviated, if not cured, through a combination of treatment and correct management.

MAREISHNESS

What is it?
A mare acts temperamentally when in season (approximately every three weeks from spring to the end of autumn).

How will it affect the horse/me?
She may seem tense and excitable, often not wanting to obey you.

How can I tell?
By seeing how she behaves when in season, both when ridden and when around other horses.

Is this the horse for me? Yes, if you are prepared to rest her or to put up with her behaviour during her seasons, or want her for breeding. However, there are now veterinary preparations available which help to reduce mareish behaviour by suppressing ovulation, and this may be worth considering if the mare is to compete a lot.

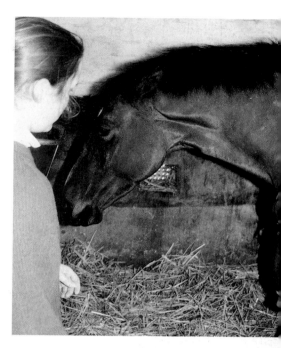

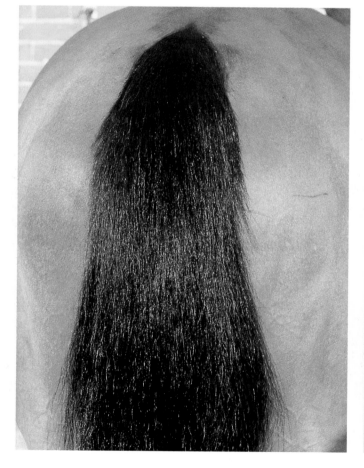

A full tail, with no signs of rubbing. If you intend to show your horse, you will need to consider a mane- and tail-rubber carefully

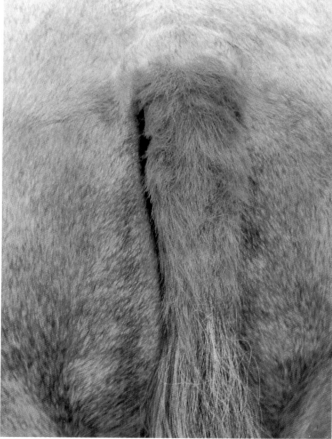

A horse that rubs its mane or tail may have an underlying condition, such as sweet itch, which causes it to rub itself sore

MOVING OFF WHEN BEING MOUNTED

What is it?
A horse that will not stand still to be mounted.

How will it affect the horse/me?
You will find it very annoying and if the horse moves off suddenly and without warning, it could cause an accident.

How can I tell?
By seeing the horse being mounted and by mounting it yourself. Don't let someone else hold the horse while you are mounting, not even on the pretext of 'just holding the stirrup for you'.

Is this the horse for me?
Probably. With patience, most horses can be taught to stand still when required. Sometimes, however, the horse's reaction to being mounted may be quite violent – it may sink to the ground, leap forwards or backwards, or to rear up – and this would not suit someone less experienced.

NAPPINESS

What is it?
A horse refuses to go away from, or pulls towards, home or other horses.

How will it affect the horse/me?
You will find it extremely frustrating, and you may not be able to get away from the yard or field at all if you are not a strong or a fairly experienced rider.

How can I tell?
By seeing the horse ridden out of the yard and away from its friends in the field or stables, and by trying it yourself.

Is this the horse for me?
Only if you have the confidence and competence to solve the problem through correct riding and schooling. Try and find out more about the nature of the nappiness: for example, if the horse is still young it may just be lacking in confidence and genuinely frightened of the big wide world; or it may refuse to go past something in particular because in the past it has been given a serious fright – a lorry, or barking dogs; perhaps its present rider is nervous and it is just 'trying it on'. *You* may be able to sort this out; though being seriously nappy for no good reason is more of a problem.

PAWING AT THE FLOOR

What is it?

The horse continually scrapes the floor of the stable or the ground when in the field.

How will it affect the horse/me?

It will wear its shoes down, and it may affect the hooves.

How can I tell?

Look at the shoes and feet. Are there signs of excessive wear at the toe? Can you see signs of scraping in the box?

Is this the horse for me?

Yes, if you can ignore the annoying noise and cope with shoeing more often. It could well be that in its present circumstances the horse is not being given enough to do and is bored; find out what his owner is doing with him, if he is let out in the field for a while each day, and then decide if you will be able to give him more stimulating work and a more varied daily routine. If you can, the pawing habit may stop.

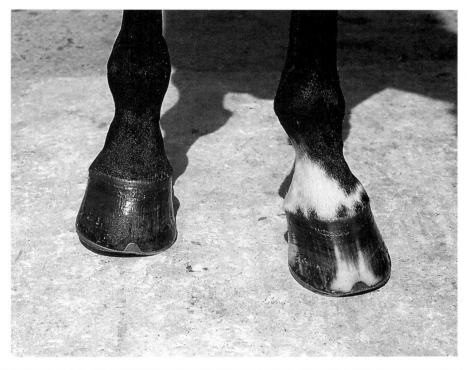

REARING

What is it?

When the horse stands up vertically on its hind legs.

How will it affect the horse/me?

The horse may fall over backwards, injuring itself and you.

How can I tell?

By seeing the horse ridden in various situations, and also by asking the owner and previous owners, if possible.

Is this the horse for me?

No. A confirmed rearer is a danger, and the habit is very hard to break – although again, try to establish the degree of the problem: if the horse gives no more than half rears, as shown in the picture, a standing martingale and strong, aggressive, forward riding may be quite enough to break the habit. Maybe the horse has been taking advantage of a lesser rider; so find out what you can, and then decide.

REFUSING TO BE LED

What is it?
A horse that pulls back, pulls you along or refuses to move when being led.

How will it affect the horse/me?
You will find it very annoying.

How can I tell?
Ask to see the horse led about the yard and around a field.

Is this the horse for me?
Only if you are confident that you can teach the horse some manners. Again, the degree of the problem is important, and how it has arisen: perhaps the horse is a dominant character and has been taking advantage of someone too nervous to cope with him. If otherwise the horse is what you want, establish if his lack of manners is only whilst leading, *then* decide if *you* have the strength of character to cope with the problem.

REFUSING TO JUMP

What is it?
When a horse stops in front of fences.

How will it affect the horse/me?
The horse will not win in competitions and may unseat you.

How can I tell?
By seeing it being jumped and by jumping it yourself.

Is this the horse for me?
Yes, if you have no jumping aspirations. No, if you want to compete seriously. It takes a very strong rider to jump clear on a horse that stops. Sometimes, however, a horse may refuse because he hurts somewhere; generally the problem is sore feet and/or a strained back, or it may be in his mouth – a sore tooth, a cut gum – or perhaps he has been jumped by a heavy-handed, lumpy rider and has entirely lost confidence. You can usually identify this sort of problem because he will appear 'footy', or he will screw his body with his ears back, or chuck his head in the air when he *does* jump. So if otherwise he is what you want, and if you want to jump but not too ambitiously, then he might still be one to consider: a thorough physical check, some remedial treatment, and sympathetic riding, may be all that is needed to restore his confidence.

RUG-TEARING

What is it?
A most costly habit in which the horse literally tears its rugs off.

How will it affect the horse/me?
It will only affect your pocket, although some horses do work themselves into a state if they cannot succeed in their task.

How can I tell?
Only by observing the horse doing it or by tell-tale little rips on a rug recently put on for your benefit. If the horse is wearing a 'bib' you should ask the seller why, as this item is used to prevent rug-tearing.

Is this the horse for me?
Yes, provided you can control the habit. Rug-tearers can often be prevented from doing so by the use of a bib, as mentioned, or more drastically with a cradle. A muzzle can also be used, although this obviously prevents the horse from eating.

SCHOOLING PROBLEMS

What is it?
A horse that does not go as desired when being schooled.

How will it affect the horse/me?
The horse will fail to build a correct topline and may become more and more confused if you don't know what to do about it.

How can I tell?
Watch the horse being schooled. Can you see what is going wrong? Ride the horse. Can you feel what is happening?

Is this the horse for me?
Yes, if all you want to do is hack out or if you are prepared to retrain the horse, either under instruction or through your own knowledge. Again, the horse's problem may be physical if he hurts somewhere – in his back, or feet, or mouth, or legs – and then he will find it very hard to perform any school movements. If he is an older horse, he may be suffering the beginnings of arthritis. For whatever purpose you want the horse, give him a thorough physical check first. Remember, too, that bad riding is often at the root of schooling problems: so if he goes much better for you than for his owner, there may not be a problem.

SHYING

What is it?
The horse jumps at objects in hedgerows or things it is unaccustomed to.

How will it affect the horse/me?
The horse may cut into itself and unseat you if you are caught unawares.

How can I tell?
By seeing the horse ridden away from home and by riding it yourself.

Is this the horse for me?
Only if you are competent and confident enough to bring the horse on. Shying is usually associated with young horses, but not exclusively so, and will not improve unless the horse can draw confidence from its rider. It may also be caused by impaired eyesight, so have its eyes tested if you are seriously considering buying.

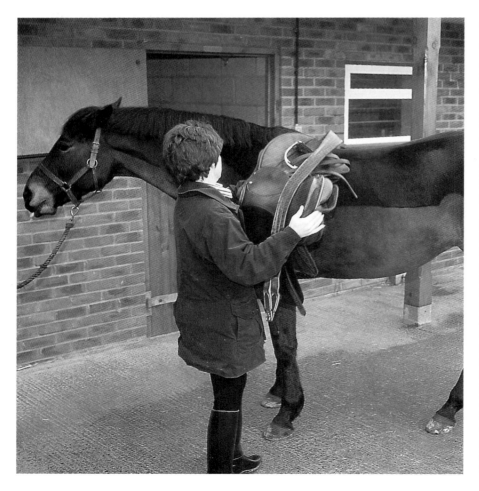

TACK-SHY

What is it?
As with a headshy horse, only this one does not like having the bridle or saddle, or both, put on.

How will it affect the horse/me?
The horse will become anxious and possibly unmanageable.

How can I tell?
By seeing the horse tacked up, and by putting on the tack yourself.

Is this the horse for me?
First try to find out why the horse is like this. Has it had a bad experience in the past, for instance? If you are fairly knowledgeable and patient, you might win its trust, but consider carefully whether you have the time for such commitment. There might also be a quite straightforward physical reason for this behaviour, for example a sore tooth or back, or damage of some sort in the mouth or saddle area, or a cut ear. Also check that the bridle and saddle fit comfortably when on; if the bit is set too high in the mouth, it will not only bruise the mouth itself, but the headpiece will pull down and bruise the tissues on the poll and at the base of the ears, and this will make a horse very nervous. A grakle fitted too tightly will have the same effect.

TEETH GRINDING

What is it?
The horse grinds its teeth when ridden in a bit and sometimes whenever it feels like it, ridden or not.

How will it affect the horse/me?
It may affect the teeth, and even the digestion if severe.

How can I tell?
By listening to the horse when it is bitted and ridden, and when in the stable.

Is this the horse for me?
Not if you are serious about dressage, as the horse will always be marked down as resisting you, and not if the noise will annoy you, as it often does. You can always, of course, wipe his front teeth with a bar of saddle soap which will generally stop him grinding them for a short while!

WEAVING

What is it?
This is when the horse rocks back and forth on its forelegs, swaying from side to side, usually over the stable door but sometimes inside the stable.

How will it affect the horse/me?
The horse may fail to thrive.

How can I tell?
Only by observing the horse doing it. At the time of purchase take note as to whether the horse has a weaving grille on its stable door – although many stables do have weaving grilles as a standard fitment, so the presence of one does not mean that the horse is definitely a weaver. However, if it seems an anxious type be sure to investigate the possibility further.

Is this the horse for me?
Not if the habit annoys you, although many weavers can be successfully controlled by the use of weaving grilles or by turning them out as much as possible. Weaving is generally the result of stress, too, so you might consider the sort of lifestyle he will have with you as compared to his present one: if this involves a great deal of competition work and travelling, being stabled all day and being highly corned up, he is much more likely to weave and display 'stress' behaviour than a horse on a lower plane of actvity and nutrition.

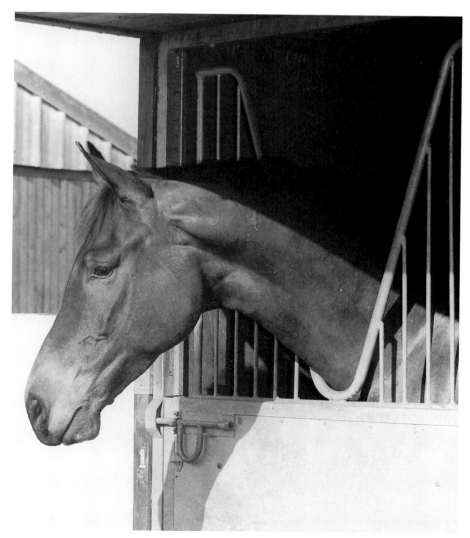

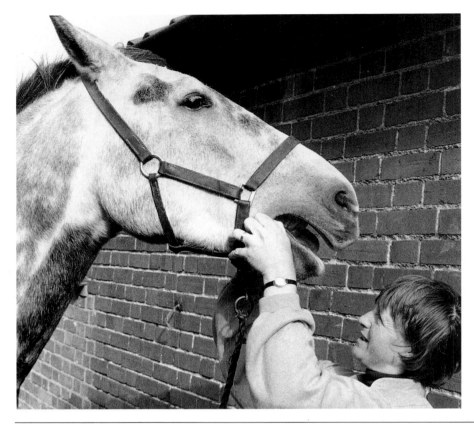

WINDSUCKING

What is it?
This is a habit in which the horse gulps in mouthfuls of air and sucks it down into its stomach, sounding rather as though it is belching.

How will it affect the horse/me?
Its teeth may become worn; it may suffer from more digestive upsets than normal; it may fail to keep weight on.

How can I tell?
Look at the teeth. Do they look bevelled? (While the horse may not need to take hold of anything in order to windsuck, it may have started off in this way and so have damaged its teeth at a younger age.) Observe the horse for some time while in the stable and out in the field. Look for any thickening of the muscle running down the throat.

Is this the horse for me?
Not if the noise gets on your nerves; not if you have other horses around, especially youngsters; probably, if it is exceptionally talented and that is all you care about.

WOOD-CHEWING

What is it?
The horse chews wood of all kinds: stable doors, fence posts, etc.

How will it affect the horse/me?
It may wear its teeth down unevenly, and it may suffer digestive upsets.

How can I tell?
Possibly through teeth wear, but usually only by seeing the horse doing it.

Is this the horse for me?
You can try to prevent the horse indulging this habit in the stable by coating the wood with a foul-tasting but non-toxic substance, and in the field through the use of electric fencing; or by running a strip of metal along the top of any wood surface where this is possible. The horse may be worth the hassle if otherwise suitable.

FAULTS OF CONFORMATION

BACK AT THE KNEE

What is it?
Where the knee appears to be behind the rest of leg, or dipping backwards.

How will it affect the horse?
It can be unsightly, but does not necessarily affect performance, although it can put extra strain on the tendons.

How can I tell?
The knees appear to bend backwards.

Is this the horse for me?
Not if showing, but otherwise yes. If the horse will be jumping a lot, however, or hunting in a hilly or heavy country, this fault may predispose it to tendon strain, particularly if it will be carrying a heavy rider.

BIG FEET

What is it?
Feet that are not in proportion to the rest of a horse's body.

How will it affect the horse?
They may not affect it at all, or they may be quite flat and therefore predispose the horse to injury such as bruised soles.

How can I tell?
Simply by observing the size of them.

Is this the horse for me?
Probably, but it would be best to discuss the problem with your farrier first. Run your hands down the horse's legs from the knee downwards to check that the size of his feet doesn't cause him to brush or cut himself; bumps and splint-like lumps and skin damage on the inside of his cannon bones could indicate a serious problem.

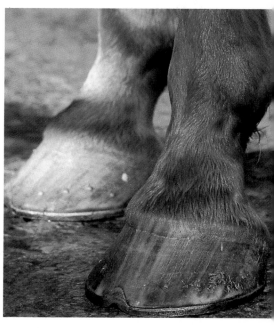

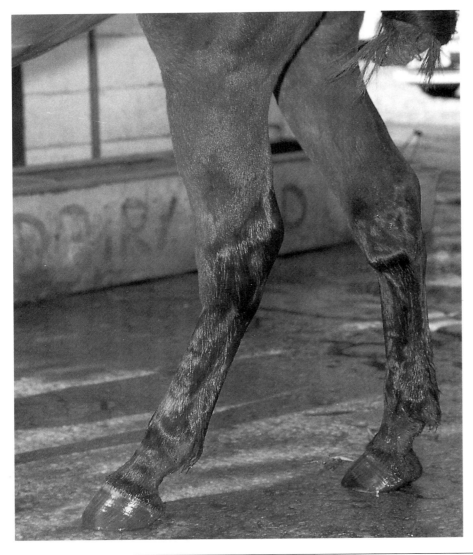

BOWED HOCKS

What is it?
The points of the hocks turn away from each other.

How will it affect the horse?
The horse will be put down the order in the show-ring. This conformation may alter its action to its disadvantage if it is required for dressage.

How can I tell?
Stand behind the horse to see whether its hocks line up straight or are placed facing away from one another.

Is this the horse for me?
Bowed hocks should not affect everyday activities but they will be a disadvantage in the show- and dressage rings. They may also compromise the horse's ability to jump well and efficiently.

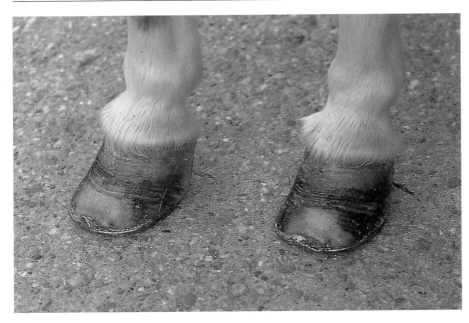

BOXY HOOVES

What is it?
Small, upright, 'tight' hooves.

How will it affect the horse?
The horse may move in a 'stilted' fashion and may be prone to conditions such as navicular.

How can I tell?
The hooves will appear small and tall.

Is this the horse for me?
Boxy feet may affect one horse and not another. Ask your veterinary surgeon's advice about having the feet X-rayed before purchase to assess possible future complications. However, although boxy feet are generally frowned upon by the cognoscenti, they do in fact often prove to be very resilient against stones and brusing.

COLD BACK

What is it?
This expression describes a horse which dips or humps its back when it is first saddled or when the rider gets on.

How will it affect the horse/me?
The horse may buck when first ridden, until it 'warms up'.

How can I tell?
By observing the horse when the saddle is fitted, or when it is first ridden.

Is this the horse for me?
A lot can be done to ease the problem, such as using a thick, comfortable numnah (saddle pad) and ensuring that the saddle is never simply dropped onto the horse's back. If the horse bucks a lot, think twice if you know you cannot cope with this at the start of every ride. The problem may also have a physical cause, or association, namely strain or damage to the back and loin muscles, so that it actually hurts the horse when you get on. So ask a back-man to check these. Also if the horse has had a rider who thumps down heavily into the saddle every time he/she gets on, it may dip its back/react adversely in anticipation of the discomfort. So establish the cause before you make a definite decision!

COW HOCKS

What is it?
The hocks are turned inwards at the points.

How will it affect the horse?
The horse may have a close action behind, and in severe cases, its hocks may even rub. However, unless it is a show animal, slight cow hocks should not affect it too much.

How can I tell?
By seeing if the points of the hocks are close together, or indeed touching. When the horse walks or trots, do its hocks rub against one another?

Is this the horse for me?
This depends on the level of competition that you are aiming for, because the higher you go in the various spheres, the more effect a peculiar action will have. As always, there are exceptions to the rule. The same arguments probably apply as for bowed hocks, in that any jumping ability may also be compromised.

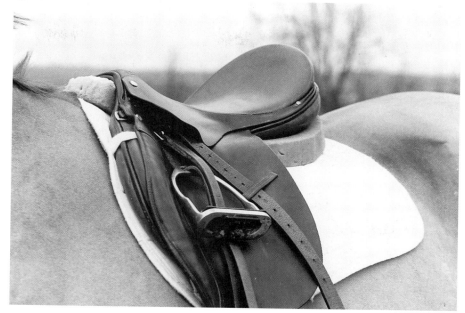

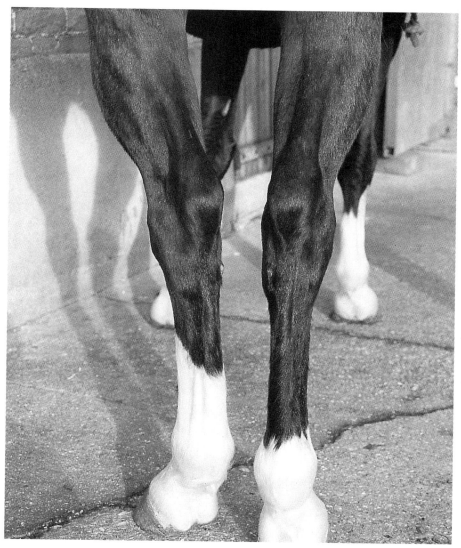

DEFORMED HOOVES

What is it?
Any deviation from a pair of well shaped hooves.

How will it affect the horse?
Poor hoof conformation may have various effects, from lameness to peculiar action.

How can I tell?
By looking at the feet and the horse's way of going.

Is this the horse for me?
Discuss the individual case with your farrier before purchase. The foot illustrated is very straight on the outside and has an outgrowing 'wing' of horn on the inside, with the result that the horse's weight is not transferred centrally down the hoof from the leg. This could lead to corns, bruising of the sole, traumatised pastern joint, even shoulder strain because any irregularity in the foot tends to have a knock-on effect right up the leg – hence the importance of the hoof being a regular, 'circular' shape.

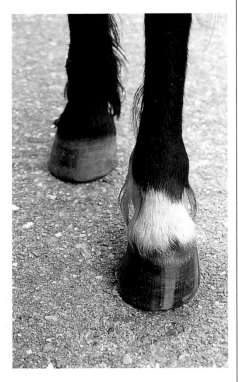

EWE NECK

What is it?
When the crest of the neck (from poll to withers) is concave rather than convex.

How will it affect the horse?
It is unsightly. The horse may tend to go hollow in the back and will be difficult to persuade into a good outline.

How can I tell?
The neck looks to be 'upside-down'.

Is this the horse for me?
Yes, if appearance does not matter and you are not interested in showing or dressage. It could also mean that the horse is awkward when it jumps.

FLAT FEET

What is it?
Feet that are splayed out and low, rather than upright.

How will it affect the horse?
The horse may suffer from cracked hooves and bruised soles quite frequently.

How can I tell?
Simply by observation.

Is this the horse for me?
Possibly. Discuss the severity of the problem with a farrier: there is no form of remedial shoeing that can significantly improve badly flat feet, and having to use leather or protective soles can cause more problems.

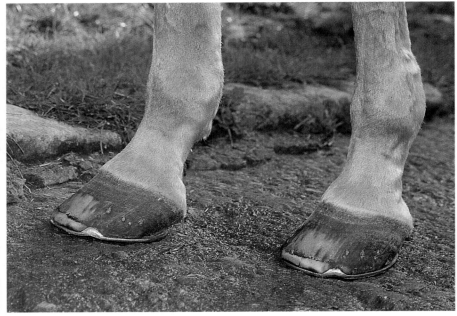

GOOSE-RUMPED

What is it?
When the slope from the highest point of the quarters runs down at an acute angle to the roots of the tail.

How will it affect the horse/me?
It is unsightly, rather than a weakness.

How can I tell?
By observing the above in the horse.

Is this the horse for me?
Yes, unless of course you are keen to go showing when this conformation will be judges less favourably against a horse with no goose rump. This shape tends to be found in lower-class animals, and sometimes in Irish-bred horses.

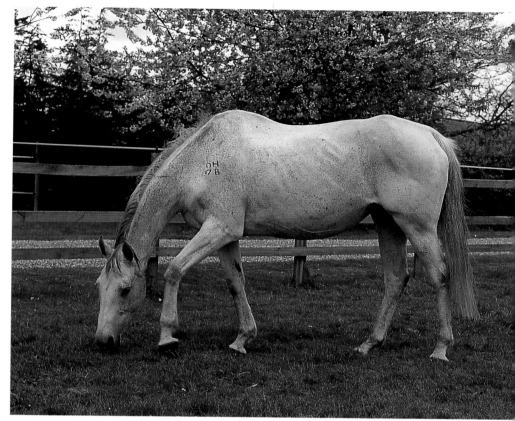

HOLLOW BACK

What is it?
When the spine seems to dip downwards more than normal.

How will it affect the horse/me?
It is a sign of weakness, as with a long back.

How can I tell?
By seeing that the spine dips down unduly. (Do not confuse this with an older horse whose back will drop with age.)

Is this the horse for me?
If you do not intend to do too much competitive work and the horse is fine in all other respects, it will probably be suitable, as long as you do not intend to do anything too arduous. Any serious weakness will have a knock-on effect to the adjoining parts, and a hollow-backed horse will never be able to use its back end to full effect; as you can see in the photo, the muscles of this horse's hindquarters are not well developed at all, and this is a direct consequence of its hollow back. It would find hill work, or a heavy country, very tiring indeed.

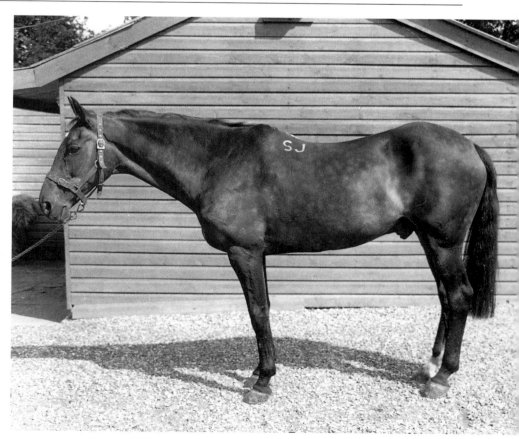

LIGHT OF BONE

What is it?
A horse that does not have the right amount of bone for the size of its body.

How will it affect the horse?
It will affect the horse's ability to carry weight.

How can I tell?
The horse will appear to have 'spindly' legs.

Is this the horse for me?
Yes, if you do not require weight-carrying ability. Ponies are often light of bone, certainly the more Thoroughbred type, but are capable of a lot of hard work; so too are Arabs, which are renowned for their endurance capabilities, and their ability to carry a man's weight for long distances.

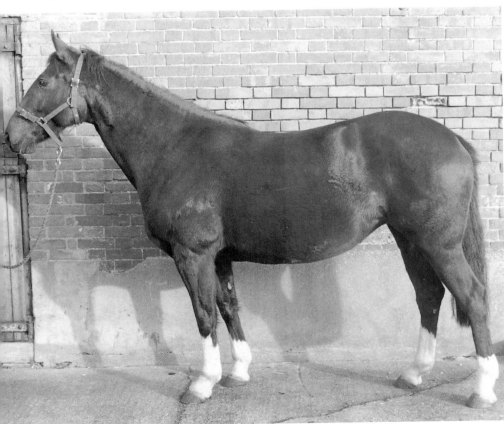

LONG BACK

What is it?
A horse with a lot of space between withers and loin area.

How will it affect the horse/me?
A long-backed horse often gives an uncomfortable ride as it creates a lot of movement. A long back can also be quite weak, not able to carry much weight.

How can I tell?
By observing the amount of space between withers and loins.

Is this the horse for me?
Probably, unless you want a lot of athletic ability or are a 'heavy' rider. It must be said that a lot of showjumpers have long backs and seem to suffer few ill effects, and that a certain amount of length in the back is essential to speed. Traditionally, breeders like to see a long back in a mare because they consider the foal *in utero* has nore room to develop.

LOP EARS

What is it?
Ears which flop down rather than standing up as normal.

How will it affect the horse?
It is unsightly.

How can I tell?
The horse seems to have a dejected appearance.

Is this the horse for me?
Providing you do not mind the appearance, yes. In fact, lop-eared horses are said to be very kind and giving.

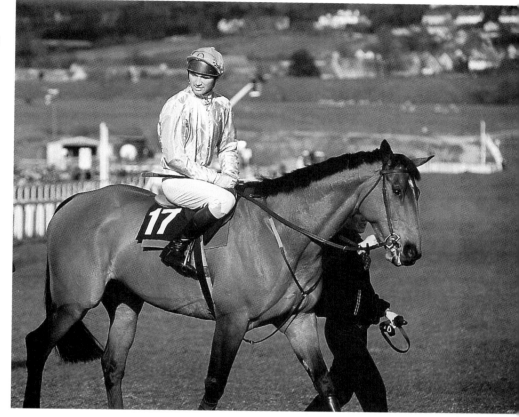

OVER AT THE KNEE

What is it?
The horse looks to be standing with its knees bent slightly forwards.

How will it affect the horse?
It may not affect it at all, but it will put a horse down the order in the show-ring. Many youngsters are 'over at the knee' but straighten up as they mature.

How can I tell?
The horse may look to be overbalancing and its knees will appear to be bulging forwards.

Is this the horse for me?
Yes, if it is fine in other respects.

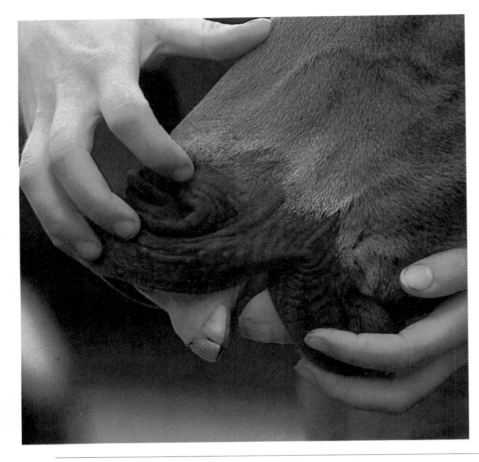

PARROT MOUTH

What is it?
The upper jaw overlaps the lower jaw.

How will it affect the horse?
It may cause problems when eating (especially grazing) or when biting.

How can I tell?
Part the horse's lips. You will see whether its teeth line up or not.

Is this the horse for me?
Unless quite severe, many parrot-mouthed horses do not suffer any ill effects. You should take your veterinary surgeon's advice on any specific case.

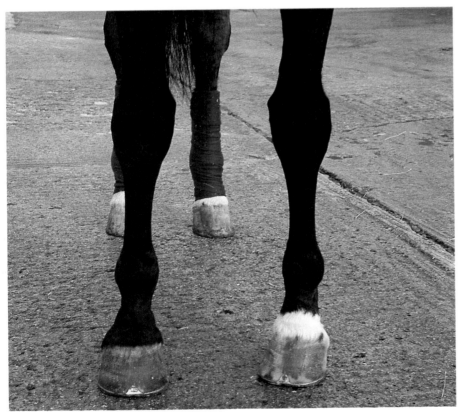

PIGEON-TOED

What is it?
The toes of the forelegs turn in towards each other.

How will it affect the horse?
The horse may move quite close in front and possibly strike into itself.

How can I tell?
Look at the horse when standing. Do its toes turn in? When observing it in trot, does it appear to be moving quite close in front?

Is this the horse for me?
Not if you want to show or take part in dressage competitions. Depending on how severe the condition is, the horse may be fine for other activities.

ROACH BACK

What is it?
When the back has an upward curve around the loin area.

How will it affect the horse/me?
The horse will not do well in the show-ring, and may give an uncomfortable, stilted ride with a short action, but it might be quite capable of jumping well.

How can I tell?
By looking at the loin area and seeing if the gradual curvature of the spine bends upwards in a bump.

Is this the horse for me?
Yes, unless you want to show, and as long as you find its ride quite comfortable.

SHORT BACK

What is it?
A horse that has a short, compact back.

How will it affect the horse/me?
A short back rarely affects a horse and is often said to be a good thing. However, a really short back may reduce the horse's capacity for speed.

How can I tell?
Simply by observing the length of the back from wither to loin. The horse will look very close and compact.

Is this the horse for me?
Yes, unless excellent conformation is of the utmost importance. Also, be sure that the horse is a comfotable ride, because a short back will sometimes give a choppy, rather jarring way of going. It also predisposes to overreach, so check the heels of the forelegs, and be suspicious of the horse is brought out for the ridden examination in overreach boots.

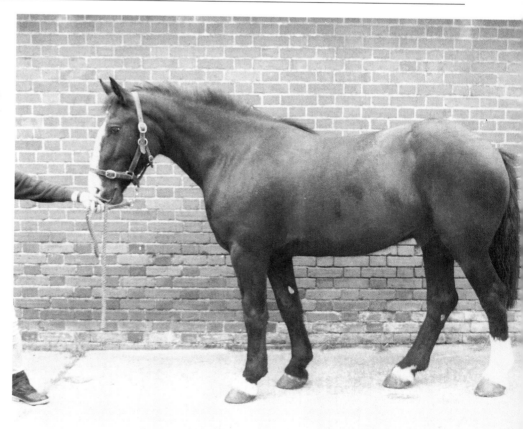

SWAY BACK

What is it?
The horse has a marked hollow due to poor skeletal conformation.

How will it affect the horse/me?
Strain will be put on the back muscles.

How can I tell?
The horse's back will seem to sag along its spine.

Is this the horse for me?
Not if you want to do more than light hacking. The pony in the photo is only young, but the problem is unlikely to resolve itself as it matures; unfortunately it will probably always be sway-backed.

TIED IN AT THE KNEE

What is it?
The leg is narrower just below the knee.

How will it affect the horse?
It is a sign of weakness in the leg. The horse may not stand up to strain.

How can I tell?
The leg looks, and is, narrower below the knee.

Is this the horse for me?
For light hacking and other light duties, but not if the horse will be expected to withstand a lot of strain.

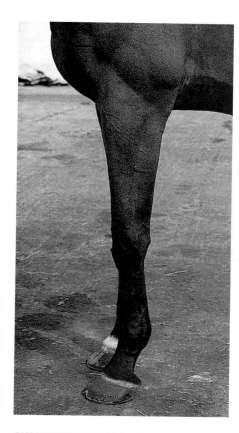

UPRIGHT PASTERNS

What is it?
Pasterns which instead of sloping gently down to the coronet, are upright so that the hooves appear to be almost underneath them.

How will it affect the horse?
This may cause jarring, and so an uncomfortable ride; it could possibly lead to unsoundness.

How can I tell?
By seeing if the pasterns appear short and upright.

Is this the horse for me?
Upright pasterns usually cause few problems, so unless you want the horse to withstand a lot of competitive work it will probably suit your purpose if it is fine in all other respects. It may give a somewhat jarring ride, on account of the extra concussion to which this conformation gives rise, particularly on a hard surface. From this increases concussion you might expect a greater tendency to windgalls, so check for these. However, neither of these constitute a serious reason *not* to buy.

UPRIGHT SHOULDER

What is it?
The shoulder blades are more upright than is desirable.

How will it affect the horse?
An upright shoulder often makes for an uncomfortable, 'choppy' ride.

How can I tell?
The horse will appear to be lacking in front, and the line where the shoulder meets the neck will be straighter than on other horses.

Is this the horse for me?
Yes, unless really good movement is important or you want a top show prospect, or if you will be riding the horse for long stretches at a time when, if it *does* give a 'choppy' ride, you will find *you* get very tired. So probably not if you want to go long-distance riding or hunting.

FAULTS DUE TO INJURY AND WEAR AND TEAR

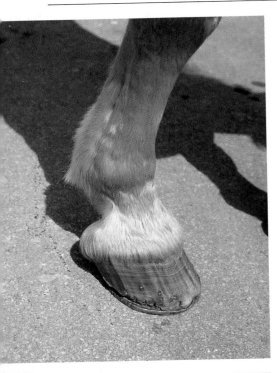

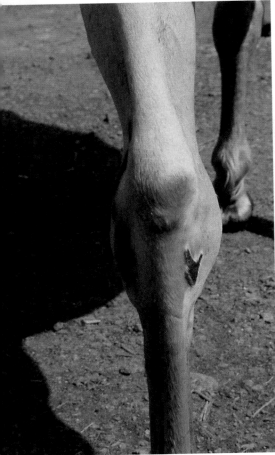

BOG SPAVIN

What is it?
Enlargement of the tibiotarsal joint capsule, clearly visible in the picture on the left.

How will it affect the horse?
The horse may be lame for a time, although often there is no lameness.

How can I tell?
Swelling can be seen around the joint; characteristically in front of the joint.

Is this the horse for me?
It may not cause problems, but this varies very much from one individual to another. Seek your veterinary surgeon's advice.

BONE SPAVIN

What is it?
A bony enlargement situated at the inner and lower part of the hock joint.

How will it affect the horse?
It may not be able to flex its hock properly and may drag its toes. It will be lame if turned sharply.

How can I tell?
You can see an enlargement on the inner and the lower part of the hock where it meets the cannon bone (see lower left photograph). Looking at the hocks from front on, they will appear to be uneven.

Is this the horse for me?
Not if you have competitive aspirations. Bone spavin cannot be cured, and the horse may become stiffer as time progresses. It is definitely classed as an unsoundness in the show-ring.

BROKEN KNEES

What is it?
Knees that have been marked where a horse has fallen on them, on the road, for example.

How will it affect the horse?
While the horse may genuinely have tripped up, broken knees could also be a sign of faulty action, and may mean that the horse trips quite frequently.

How can I tell?
It will have marks on its knees.

Is this the horse for me?
See how the horse goes during a trial. Does it seem to trip and stumble a lot? Ask the owner outright why it has scars. Consider not buying the horse if the owner will not let you have it on trial, or at least let you ride it a few times at his/her premises.

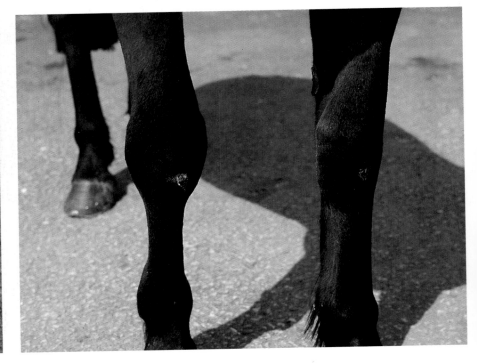

CAPPED ELBOW

What is it?
A hardening of the flesh around the point of the elbow.

How will it affect the horse?
It is unsightly, but nothing more.

How can I tell?
Feel the point of the elbow. You will detect a hard lump that you can move about.

Is this the horse for me?
Yes, unless you intend to show at top-class level.

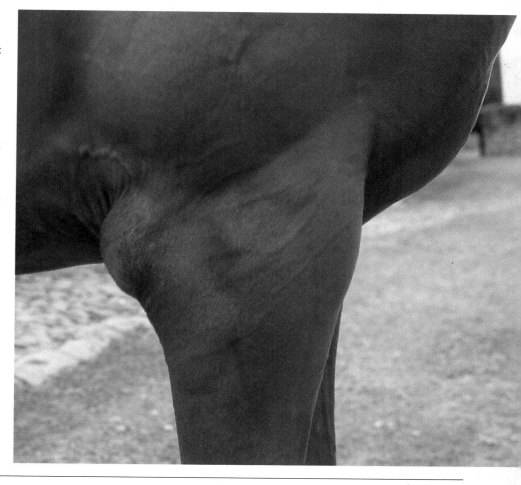

CAPPED HOCK

What is it?
A swelling at the point of the hock which, once it has been sustained, is permanent.

How will it affect the horse/me?
It will put the horse down the order in the show-ring, but otherwise does not affect its soundness.

How can I tell?
Look at both hocks. Does one or both look enlarged? Study other horses if you are not sure.

Is this the horse for me?
Yes, provided you do not care about showing, and even with such a blemish, if the horse is a real winner a capped hock may not prove too disastrous.

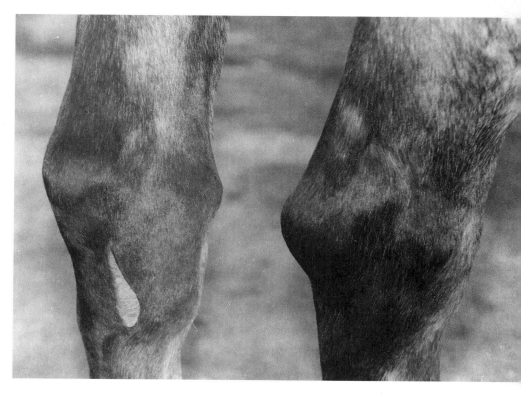

CRACKED HOOVES

What is it?
Cracks in the hoof wall.

How will it affect the horse?
Unless very bad these should not affect the horse, although they can be unsightly.

How can I tell?
You can see cracks in the hoof wall.

Is this the horse for me?
Yes, but discuss the condition with your farrier before purchase, especially if the cracks are bad.

CURB

What is it?
A true curb is the result of a sprain of the ligament at the back of the hock, and is due to faulty conformation. A false curb is a fault of confirmation; it is generally congenital.

How will it affect the horse?
A true curb may not affect the horse until later in its life, when it may appear to show 'arthritic' symptoms.

How can I tell?
When standing at right-angles to the hocks you will notice a small, or it may be larger, lump on the back of one or other or both of the hocks, fairly low down.

Is this the horse for me?
True curbs are a sign of weakness and they may degenerate. Ask your veterinary surgeon's opinion on individual cases.

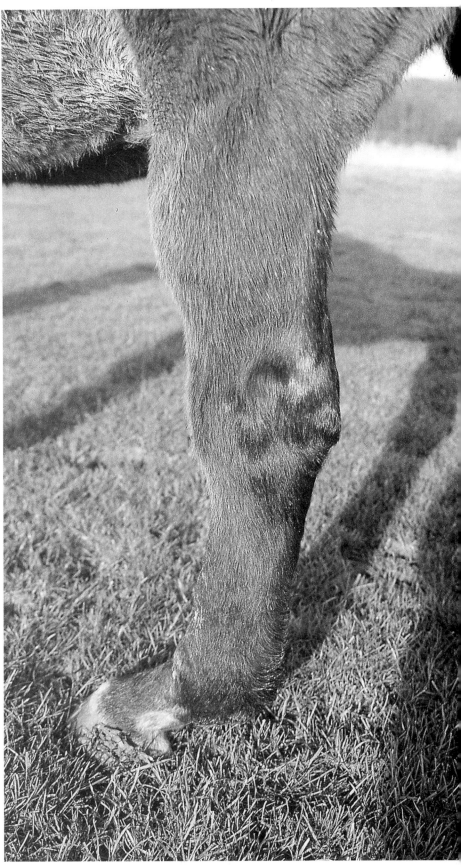

RINGBONE

What is it?
A bony formation which, if situated around the pastern is called high ringbone, and if affecting the bones in the hoof, low ringbone.

How will it affect the horse?
The horse may start off being only slightly lame, but this will become more consistent as the condition progresses.

How can I tell?
You will be able to feel bony enlargements if you run your hand down the front of the horse's leg.

Is this the horse for me?
No, the condition can only deteriorate.

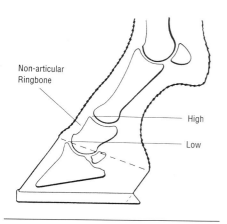

Non-articular Ringbone

High

Low

SIDEBONE

What is it?
An ossification of the lateral cartilages of the bone of the foot.

How will it affect the horse?
The horse may be lame quite a lot.

How can I tell?
It may seem to be 'footy' and you may be able to feel enlargements above the coronet.

Is this the horse for me?
No, as it is likely to suffer from chronic lameness in the future, if not sooner.

SPLINT

What is it?
A bony growth which forms between the splint bone and the cannon bone in either the fore- or hind limbs, but most commonly in the forelimbs.

How will it affect the horse?
While they are forming in younger horses the horse may go lame, but once 'set', they seldom cause problems.

How can I tell?
You can see and feel bumps on the inside of the bones of the lower legs.

Is this the horse for me?
Yes, but take your veterinary surgeon's opinion on problematic ones.

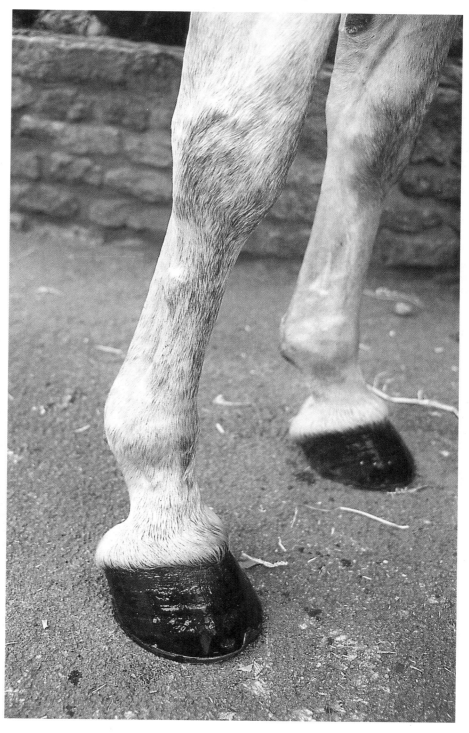

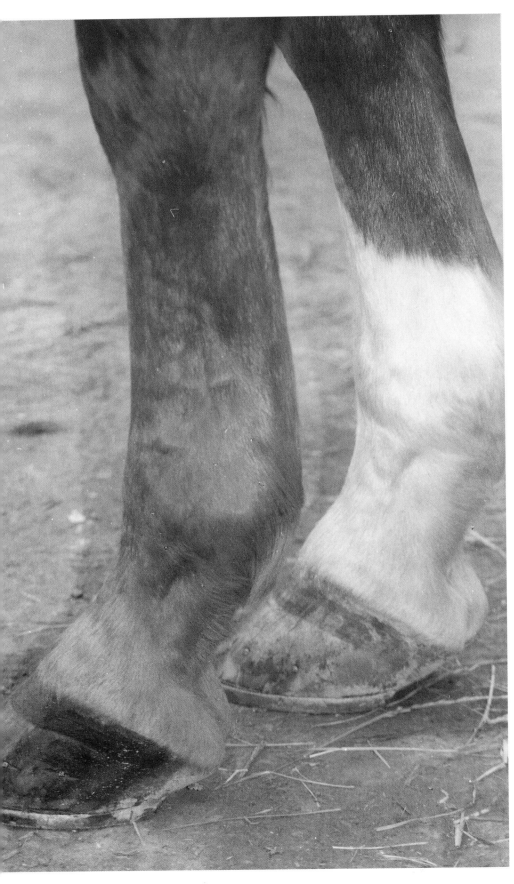

STRINGHALT

What is it?
A nervous complaint which causes the horse to snatch up its hock spasmodically. It may happen occasionally or persistently, almost as an extension of the horse's movement. The condition may deteriorate.

How will it affect the horse?
It is unsightly but does not necessarily affect performance in any given sphere except for showing and dressage.

How can I tell?
Watch the hind legs when the horse is moving: you will see it snatch up one hock while the other moves normally, although sometimes both hocks are affected.

Is this the horse for me?
This depends upon personal choice and whether or not the horse is to be shown. It also depends upon how well the horse appears to tolerate its problem.

TENDON DAMAGE

What is it?
The tendons of the legs have been damaged by strain or injury (more often the forelegs).

How will it affect the horse?
The horse will be extremely lame and the tendons will never recover to their former state.

How can I tell?
You will see a thickening down the back of one or both of the fore- or hind legs.

Is this the horse for me?
Not unless you feel confident that the horse will stand up to your requirements if you are seeking to compete. Such a horse may prove eminently suitable for hacking, but this condition should be reflected in the sale price. Having said this, many horses with thickened tendons will hunt and jump for several years – but the condition constitutes a risk.

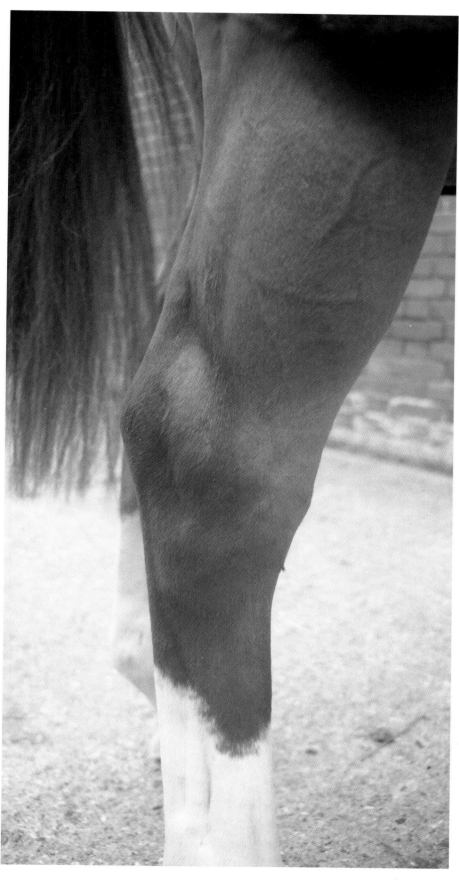

THOROUGHPIN

What is it?
A distension of the tendon sheath, seen as a fluid mass above and on either side of the hock.

How will it affect the horse/me?
Only in showing.

How can I tell?
By feeling just in front and above the point of the hock. The swelling will feel soft and may be pushed from side to side of the hock.

Is this the horse for me?
Yes, providing you do not want to do top-level showing.

WINDGALL

What is it?
A bursal enlargement which can be of varying size, round the fetlock joint.

How will it affect the horse?
It rarely causes lameness, but it may affect a judge's opinion in the show-ring if it is pronounced.

How can I tell?
You will see puffy swelling appear on either side of the joint; this may reduce after work.

Is this the horse for me?
Yes, unless you are aiming for high-level showing.

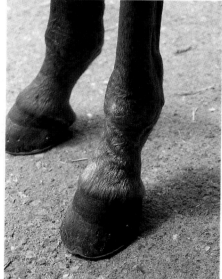

HONESTY IS THE KEY

Elizabeth found herself in a real dilemma. She wanted to sell Milly, her much loved horse, but knew that if she disclosed that it was a crib-biter she would have to reduce the mare's price drastically, which she could not afford to do. In the end she decided to advertise the mare without disclosing the vice, and would then see how she felt when any potential buyers came along.

The first people to try the horse said she was not suitable, so the question did not arise. The second people were very interested, but did not even ask Elizabeth about vices, so she did not mention it. However, when the horse was vetted, the vet picked up the 'ground' appearance on the horse's front teeth and asked Elizabeth point blank whether the horse was a crib-biter. She told him the truth.

The potential buyers called Elizabeth that evening and were very annoyed. They felt she had duped them and cost them a vetting fee unnecessarily. She did feel bad, especially as the buyers called her a cheat and a liar. As a week had gone by since the advertisement, Elizabeth then had to re-advertise Milly, a cost she would rather have done without. This time she decided not to tell people over the telephone about the crib-biting, but to inform them if they appeared to like Milly. This she did and the two buyers who were interested both tried to drop the price. They liked the horse but were simply not prepared to pay top money for her as the vice would affect any resale value. Elizabeth had other people wanting to view so she did not make any decision and consequently lost the sale.

A young girl called Sarah then came to see Milly, and liked her very much. They really did suit each other and Elizabeth was dreading having to tell her about the crib-biting. The longer she left it the harder it became, but the minute Sarah mentioned having the horse vetted, Elizabeth had to come clean. She could not believe her ears when Sarah turned round and said 'Oh, that doesn't matter, my old pony crib-bites and you couldn't get a better pony than him. We have boarded all the walls of his stable flat and use electric fencing in the field so he simply cannot crib-bite. Milly will be all right kept with him.'

Elizabeth still keeps in touch with Sarah and Milly, and is delighted that they have done really well together eventing.

MORAL *Always be honest about your horse, otherwise as well as being unfair on unsuspecting buyers, you will cause yourself a lot of hassle and worry. There is always a right person for any horse, you might just have to be a little more patient before he or she comes along.*

5
EXAMINATION PROCEDURE

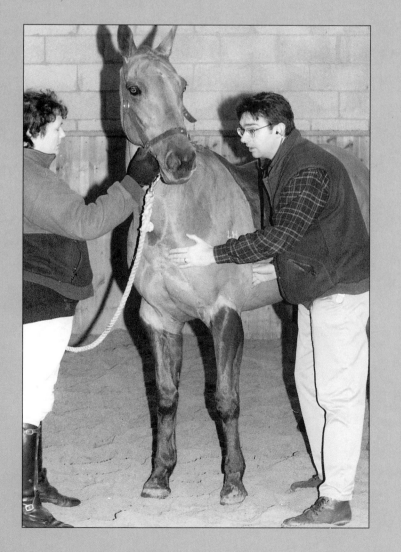

THE VET'S ROLE

Having found your ideal horse, there is one last major obstacle to overcome before you can take possession of it, and that is to have it vetted. It is essential that you use a good horse vet for this job, so ask any horsy friends you may have if they can recommend one. Small animal veterinary surgeons tend not to have the experience or specialist knowledge required to offer an opinion on a horse's suitability for a given purpose, so take the trouble to find an appropriate vet. While many sellers may offer to arrange to find a vet for you, do not take up their offer. It may be genuine, and so will be the vet who attends the horse through the seller, but if the seller is a good customer, the vet will, if only subconsciously, be on his or her side. You must have the vet working on your behalf alone.

Also be wary if the seller informs you that he/she has a current veterinary certificate. Again, this may be a perfectly genuine matter, so ask the seller to show it to you and note the details of the attending vet so that you can give them a call to discuss it. However, you do not know for what purpose the horse was vetted, so take

your own vet's advice before proceeding with any purchase.

When you ask a vet to carry out a pre-purchase examination, he is obliged to give his expert opinion regarding the suitability of the horse for the purpose intended. Such examinations are not cheap, costing (in the UK) between £100–£150 (1996), but they do offer a measure of reassurance and will protect you against the mistake of buying an unhealthy or totally unsuitable horse. However, if the first horse you consider buying fails the vet, you may soon become less inclined to have such an examination repeated, especially if the next horse you look at, and even the following one, also fail. Nonetheless, no matter how sure you are that you have found the exact horse for you, you really should have it vetted for your own safety and peace of mind.

While many unsuccessful buyers – and sellers – would argue to the contrary, vets really do want to be able to recommend purchase, so are constantly looking for the horse's good, as well as bad, qualities. This is why there is actually no such thing as a horse 'passing' a veterinary examination. While

the vet will obviously report any major findings such as lameness or heart defects, his main task is to advise you whether the horse is suitable for what you intend to do with it. Therefore it is possible for a vet to 'fail' a horse for one potential purchaser and 'pass' it for another. Should the vet advise against purchase, ask him to state the reasons, and make sure you understand what he is talking about. This may help you to avoid getting as far as an examination for another horse with similar inadequacies. If you are aware of a problem but are still thinking of buying, then give your vet as many details as you possibly can before the examination is carried out. This way he can assess the situation, giving full consideration to your needs and personal indifferences.

It is certainly a good idea for you to be present at the examination so that any possible problems can be brought to your immediate attention and discussed there and then. However, it is still common practice for the veterinary surgeon to go away and prepare his report before he will give you his full recommendations.

TYPES OF VETERINARY EXAMINATION

There are two types of pre-purchase veterinary examination, both of which are quite standard and methodical procedures. The first is a short two-stage investigation, the second consists of five stages. Both are intended to aid the identification of clinical signs of injury or disease and most vets will follow a detailed procedure as laid down by their national veterinary association. In the UK, most veterinary surgeons will follow the joint recommendations of the British Veterinary Association and the Royal College of Veterinary Surgeons. In the USA, veterinarians have to answer to the American Veterinary Medical

Association, and also the American Association of Equine Practitioners.

Which type of examination is carried out will depend upon the horse's age, the purpose for which it is intended and the asking price. As a general rule, most horses undergo the full five-stage process, unless the following points apply, when the short vetting will probably be deemed more appropriate:

■ where the horse is still too young to be ridden;

■ where the asking price is comparatively low;

■ where the purpose for which the horse is intended is of an easy nature, such as light hacking or as a companion horse.

A short vetting generally consists of just the first two stages of the full five-stage examination as detailed in the following pages. The examination is just as thorough, checking the basic soundness of wind, limb, body and vision. However, it does not set out to determine problems that may present themselves during or after exercise, as the horse is not ridden or exercised for the examination.

FIVE-STAGE EXAMINATION

STAGE ONE – PRELIMINARY EXAMINATION

The order in which a vet carries out such an examination may vary, but it will generally follow a pattern similar to that which follows.

- Upon entering the stable, the first thing the vet will do is to stand back in order to get an overall impression of the horse. He or she will determine its approximate size, look for any obvious conformational faults, and will generally assess the horse's character.

- Next he will run his hands over the horse from head to tail, noting any defects such as splints, blemishes or skin disorders. The feet will be picked up in turn so that their shape and condition can be assessed.

- He will then look at the horse's teeth to determine its age, which can be judged quite accurately up to the age of ten, but gets progressively more difficult thereafter.

- Its eyes will then be examined with an instrument called an ophthalmoscope which enables the vet to detect signs of vision impairment.

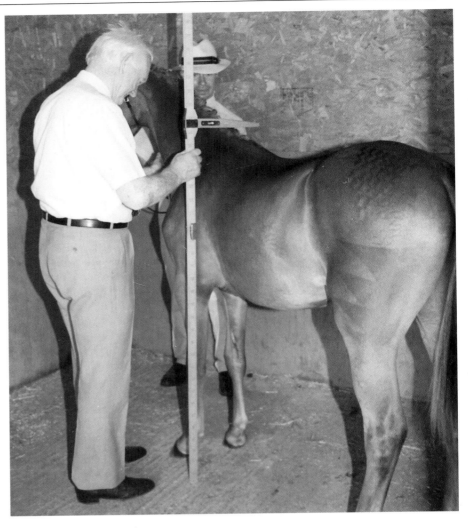

If you need to know the horse's 'exact' height, ask your veterinary surgeon to measure this at the pre-purchase examination. Otherwise he will just give an approximate height

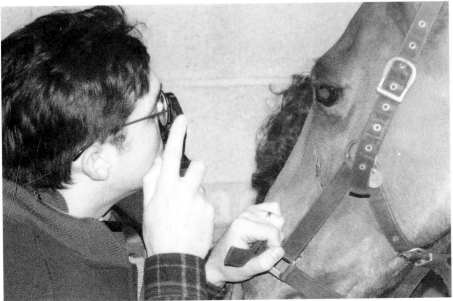

The initial stage of vetting is carried out in the stable, where the vet gives the horse a thorough examination; here he inspects the eye

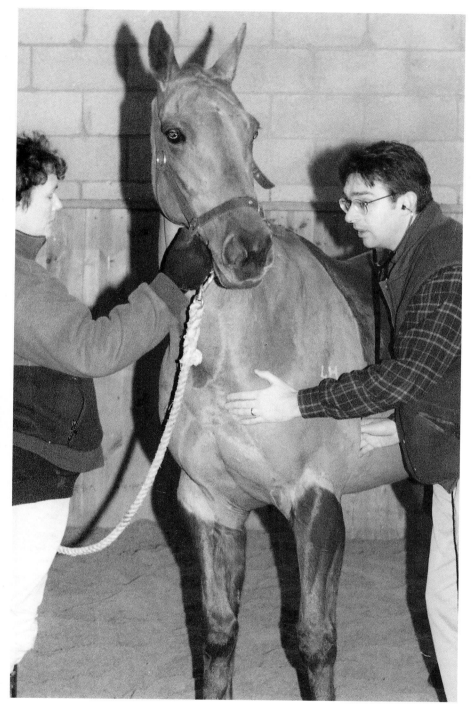

out flexion tests but most do perform them. Each leg is 'flexed' by being held up for about 45–60 seconds, then immediately the leg is released, the horse is trotted on. Many horses will show a few 'hoppy' strides after this is done, but they will soon regain their natural movement. Prolonged stiff or lame strides indicate a problem. Flexion tests on the hock may show up signs of bone spavin, while low flexion tests on the fetlock joint may show up signs of navicular. Such tests fall into the 'grey area' of veterinary experience, rather than clear-cut clinical signs. All vets can detect splints, for example, but determining a problem from the horse's movement after a flexion test takes an experienced horse vet.

He will check the horse's heart for defects; the pulse rate will also provide a yard-stick by which to compare the readings taken later, after exercise

He will flex all four legs in turn and make the horse trot away immediately; this will reveal any stiffness in the joints (more likely in an older animal), or any signs of pain

- While the horse is resting, the vet will listen to its heart and lungs with a stethoscope; the 'resting' values obtained will provide a guide which he can compare to values noted after exercise.

- He will then have the horse led outside where he can take another look at it in a better light. Should he find

anything at this stage of the examination which leads him to believe that the horse is not fit for your purpose, such as a heart or limb defect, the examination will be terminated.

- The horse's limbs will then be 'flexed' (known as a flexion test) to determine any signs of pain or movement restriction. Not all vets agree with carrying

STAGE TWO – TROTTING OUT

In order to assess correct movement and soundness, the vet will require the horse to be walked away and then back towards him, then trotted away and back again. He will advise the handler to keep a slack lead-rope so that the horse may have the freedom to show its natural paces, quite uninhibited by the handler.

For this phase of the examination a hard, flat, even surface is required. In the absence of a suitable area for trotting up in the yard, it has been known for the vet to stop traffic on a lane or road nearby, so be prepared for this!

Few horses appear lame at walk unless it is very severe, so the vet will always scrutinise the horse in trot, perhaps asking for it to be trotted up again, and yet again if there is any doubt. Should the horse appear unsound, the examination will be stopped.

There may be an obvious cause for the lameness, such as an injury, and while you might find it extremely annoying that the seller did not inform you of this problem beforehand, there is little you can do but ask your vet to return once the horse has recovered.

All being well, the vet may ask to see the horse trotted in circles on a hard surface to determine whether there appears to be any pain in the lower limbs. Providing your vet is happy with the horse's soundness, he will proceed to the next stage of the vetting process.

The vet will want to see the horse trotted up on a good, even surface, both towards and away from him; the person leading the horse will be told to keep the lead-rope slack so that he/she doesn't support it or influence its natural movement in any way

Next, the vet needs to assess how the horse copes with physical stress, and to do this he will want it exercised and to be worked quite hard at canter, and then at a controlled gallop. He will want it to pass quite close to him on the completion of each circuit, so that he can listen to its breathing; he will be looking out for any signs of stress, and for any abnormal sounds that would indicate breathing difficulties

STAGE THREE – STRENUOUS EXERCISE

This stage is performed in order to determine problems that only become apparent during or after exercise. Having had a good indication of the condition of the horse's heart and lungs while at rest, the vet now wants to see how it copes with stress.

While the aim is to exert the horse to such an extent that its breathing becomes deep and the action of its heart increases, the vet will not want it to be exerted to the point of complete exhaustion. In general, the average riding horse will reach a sufficient stage of activity after about eight to ten minutes of controlled canter, when the vet will then ask for it to be pushed into a con-

trolled gallop. He will stand close to the edge of the arena, or on a point on the circuit where the horse passes near to him, so that he can assess its breathing throughout.

The horse's age and state of fitness will always be taken into account. For instance, an event horse will require quite a lot of work for assessment, while an unfit cob will require little in comparison. A young horse not yet backed will be put on the lunge and trotted round unless only a short vetting is being carried out.

Once the horse has been stressed enough, the vet will listen to its heart and lungs with the stethoscope. While it was being worked, he will also have assessed whether it showed any signs of stiffness or lameness.

STAGE FOUR –
PERIOD OF REST

After exercise the horse is returned to its box where it will be allowed to rest for about 30 minutes. During this time the vet will observe its breathing and check its heart rate to see how quickly they return to the 'resting' values which were measured at the start.

While the horse is left to relax, the vet may use this time to fill out its description chart, noting any white markings, whorls or other distinguishing marks.

STAGE FIVE –
FOOT EXAMINATION AND
SECOND TROT-UP

Using pincers or hoof testers, the vet will inspect the horse's hooves, looking for sensitive or diseased areas. Should anything give him reason to believe that there is a problem, he may ask to remove the horse's shoes for a closer examination.

Providing he is still satisfied with the horse's state of health, he will repeat stage two. He will also ask for the horse to be turned in tight circles on both reins and backed up. This is done in order to show any stiffness after exercise. For instance, a problem in the hind leg area may mean the horse cannot back up or cross its hind legs without obvious signs of discomfort.

During this final stage, the vet will satisfy himself that the horse's heart and breathing rates have returned completely to normal.

Having completed his examination, the vet may give you some indication of his opinion, but he will still wish to go away and write up his vetting certificate before finally expressing his favour or disapproval of purchase.

At the end of the day the vet's report simply indicates that he has found no sign of abnormality, disease or injury other than those recorded in the document. Should any problems that *were* found be significant enough to sway the vet's opinion against purchase, he will tell you why; but all being well, he will be able to inform you that, in his opinion, the conditions that he found will not affect the horse's suitability for what you want to do with it.

OPINION OR GUARANTEE?

The important word here is 'opinion'. No vet gives a 'guarantee' that the horse is definitely suitable, or free from any abnormality. However, he does have an obligation to ensure that his opinion is sound, and furthermore, should the horse develop some condition that should have been apparent at the vetting, he can be found negligent. However, price, height, suitability for your own riding ability, breeding status and temperament are all issues between yourself and the purchaser, as is the matter of vices. The vet may feel that he has a moral responsibility to protect a child or perhaps a person with a disability from purchasing a horse which is obviously too much for them to handle, but if the animal is otherwise fit and healthy, all he can do is to bring the matter of suitability to the attention of both parties, allowing you to make your own decision.

At the end of the day, by having a horse vetted you are simply reducing the risk of buying a 'wrong 'un'. It may prove costly in the short term, but in the long term it is essential.

SPECIAL EXAMINATIONS

During a routine examination the vet will not undertake special examinations that may be desirable for the horse's intended purpose unless you specifically request him to do so. These special examinations will involve extra cost but may safeguard you if you are buying for a specific purpose; for example, you want to breed from the horse, or event at Advanced level. Further examinations that you may consider would include the ones described below.

Blood tests

In the interests of all parties it is always a good idea to have your vet take a routine blood sample during the examination. It protects the seller, in that they cannot later be accused of drugging the horse in any way; it protects the buyer in that, should a problem occur within a few weeks of purchase, the blood can then be analysed for malpractice, for example, the horse was given drugs to mask a problem; and it protects the vet in that if a problem occurs later, he cannot be accused of negligence should any evidence of a cover-up on the part of the seller be revealed.

Often two samples are taken, one for immediate analysis, the other to be retained for a period of up to three weeks. The one for immediate analysis can provide valuable information on the horse's state of health, such as a nutrient deficiency or evidence of worm infestation. However, your vet will only check for such things if you ask him to, so if you want this information be sure to do so. The other sample can be used, if necessary, to determine whether the horse was given something to mask any pain, perhaps because of lameness; some form of sedative to calm a nervous or neurotic disposition; or something to mask breathing problems such as chronic obstructive pulmonary disease. With the evidence of a blood test taken at the time, you will have concrete proof of a cover-up; without a blood test you have nothing. No seller should object to a routine blood sample being taken, and if he or she does, alarm bells should start to ring.

X-rays

Where a horse's price is quite substantial, or where the horse is destined for high-level competition, your vet may recommend the X-raying of its limbs and feet, and this may also be an insurance requirement for such horses. A conformation problem such as one hoof being smaller than the other, or bony enlarge-

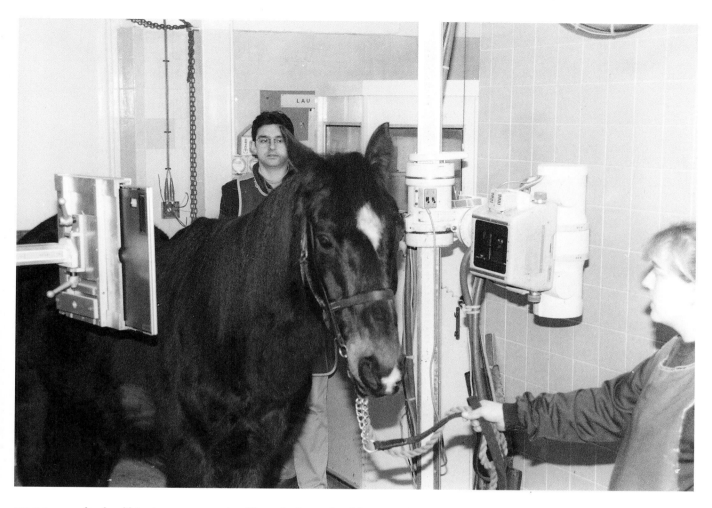

Here the horse's withers are being X-rayed as the veterinary surgeon detected a possible problem during the pre-purchase examination which he wanted confirmed before he advised against purchase

ments, may also lead him to recommend this procedure for a fairly standard horse. Interpreting X-rays can be quite a complicated job, so again, it takes an experienced eye to decide what may be important and what can be ignored. X-rays are, of course, limited to recording past events and this can be detrimental to the purchase of a suitable horse. For instance, X-rays might show up a past injury which may not have bothered the horse in years and may never do so for the rest of its life. However, the knowledge that it is there does tend to put a little doubt in your mind. In my opinion, X-rays should only be performed if a problem is suspected or if they are an insurance requirement, not as a routine pre-purchase procedure.

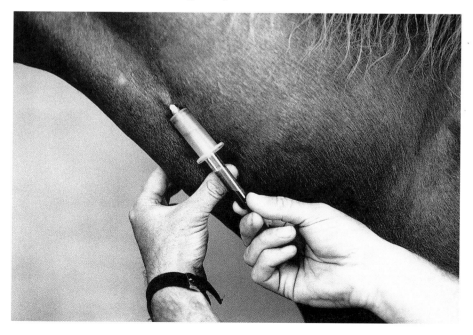

Taking a blood sample

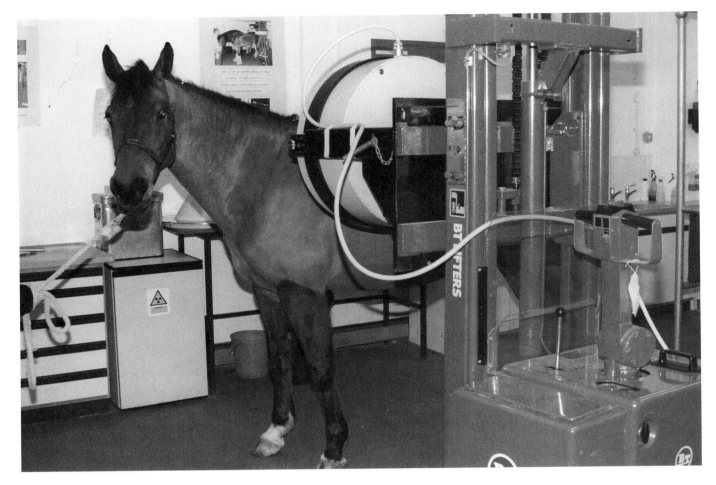

Ultrasound scans

The need for ultrasound scanning may be indicated where a tendon or ligament injury is suspected. Additionally, in the case of a competition horse, you might want to satisfy yourself that there have been no past injuries which have healed without any external trace. However, as with X-rays, ultrasound scans can be difficult to interpret, and are generally only performed where a problem has already been found in order to obtain an idea of the extent of the damage and a forecast for future soundness.

Endoscoping

When a horse has been heard to 'make a noise' (inspiratory noises heard during the period of exertion), endoscoping may help to establish the cause. The vet will want to ascertain whether the horse has a temporary condition such as an infection, or a permanent one such as a partial laryngeal paralysis. Such a procedure will also help to establish whether or not the horse has been operated on, for example it may have been Hobdayed.

The examining vet may advise ultrasound scanning where a past tendon or ligament injury is suspected, or a bone change where there are no external signs of damage

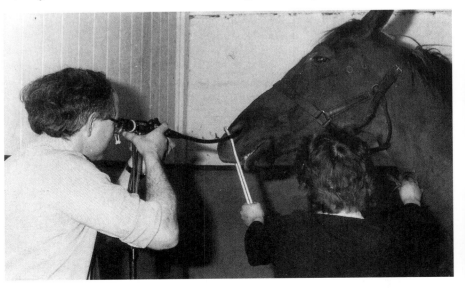

Horse undergoing an endoscopic investigation

SUITABILITY FOR THE PURPOSE INTENDED

So far we have heard quite a lot about 'suitability for the purpose intended' – so what exactly does this statement mean, and whose job is it to ensure that the horse is suitable? When buying a horse, there are two main factors we have to look at:

■ the ability of the person/rider who will be handling the horse;
■ the ability of the horse for a given purpose.

Matching the ability of the rider/handler with the right type of horse is the responsibility of the new owner. If you are sensible, you will employ the help of an experienced person to ease your decision, but at the end of the day *you* must be the one to decide whether or not you feel able to cope with the type of horse you are intending to buy.

Matching the ability of the horse to the purpose intended is a joint decision between owner and vet. As the potential new owner, you should satisfy yourself that the horse has the athletic ability, looks or temperament to be a willing partner for your intentions. If it is for dressage, then you should be sure that it moves suitably well and has the sort of conformation you require; if it is to show, then you must assess the horse's conformation and build for the appropriate category; and if all you want is to hack out and have a good time with it, then it is up to you to make sure that its temperament and behaviour are appropriate. You should assess the horse's suitability in this way long before you even call your vet with a

'Suitability for the purpose intended' not only refers to the ability of the horse for a given job, but also to the ability of the rider. It is your responsibility to ensure you can cope with, and make the best use of the horse you are intending to buy

view to a pre-purchase examination. The ideal time to call him is when you are sure that this is the horse for you, and are firmly hoping that he will recommend purchase.

Do not expect the vet to come out and make the decision for you. His job is simply to assess whether the horse's state of health will withstand the life it will be leading with you. As well as examining what he sees before him on the day, the vet will also be looking for signs of past injury or disease which could affect your purpose. Should he find any defects (which is highly likely because no horse is perfect, and the vet is looking for anything which strays from normal), his task is then to evaluate the severity of these defects with regard to your specific needs.

The point cannot be stressed enough that the vet is vetting the horse for *your particular needs*. Should the defects be only minor, the vet may list them on the pre-purchase certificate just to point out that he has seen them, but he may see little reason to discuss them with you in any great detail. If he feels the defects found may have some bearing on your purpose, either present or future, he will discuss their implications fully and then arrive at a decision on purchase with you. Should he feel that the defects will most certainly have a detrimental effect regarding your purpose, he will advise against purchase.

You have to remember that, as well as working on your behalf, a vet is also looking to safeguard himself. He will not take any chances on a horse, as you, the potential purchaser, might. Should he advise purchase with the knowledge that a particular condition *may* affect the horse, he is leaving himself open to legal action should things go wrong. Out of necessity, therefore, the vet's decision is always on the cautious side.

IGNORING VETERINARY ADVICE

In view of this caution, you may be tempted to disregard your vet's advice. After all, the horse seemed fine when you rode it, and your adviser could find nothing physically wrong with it, so perhaps your vet is being somewhat 'over'-cautious. If you are thinking along these lines, the best advice I can give to you is: 'Think very, very carefully before ignoring your vet's advice, unless you have more knowledge than he does.' You certainly would think twice about buying a house after a surveyor had informed you that it was likely to fall down, no matter how appealing or how perfect its location. Providing you have informed the vet of your 'exact' requirements, you *should* take his advice. He is giving you the benefit of his vast experience in such matters, so if you do not intend to abide by his decision, do not waste your money by having the horse vetted in the first place.

Second opinions

If, having read the preceding paragraph, you are still convinced that this is the horse for you, and you will not be swayed from your decision, you may want to look further into the reasons given against purchase. First, talk to the vet again, explain why the horse means so much to you, and ask what, if anything, might be done about the problems. Is it simply a case of money being needed to treat the horse, or will it have long-term problems? Most vets will be willing to go to such lengths of discussion, especially if they can see that you have a real desire to own this particular horse, for whatever reason. You may find that there is some hope if you are willing to compromise in some way – perhaps by not jumping the horse, for example – but in all honesty, if you told your vet originally that you wanted to jump, then it's because that's precisely what you want to do! There will be another horse which will suit you, so why tie yourself to one that is less than what you were looking for?

If your vet seems reluctant to discuss the matter any further, you may wish to talk to another vet within another practice. While they may be willing to discuss the problems briefly, they will have to see the horse in order to offer a second opinion, and this will, of course, involve another pre-purchase examination fee. It is a good idea to tell the second vet what was found to be wrong with the horse, but do not give him the first vet's name, simply because you should not be out to cause any ill feeling between rival practices. Similarly, do not report back to the first vet with an 'I told you so' attitude if the horse is subsequently passed for purchase.

THE LAST WORD

If there is any doubt about the suitability of the horse for your purpose, due to health defects, lack of ability or simply because of a peculiarity you cannot define, do not buy it. It will cost you just as much to keep the wrong horse as the right one. Be sensible: take your vet's advice and you will have many years of pleasure with the right horse, once found.

VALUE YOUR VET'S VIEWS

Tim Smith had found what he thought to be the perfect horse in George, a dark bay, eight-year-old, 16.2hh gelding. George was a good all-rounder and had hunted for the past two seasons, something which Tim wanted to do. He knew he should have the horse vetted, but was reluctant to do so because he did not want anything to be wrong. However, good sense won through and so he instructed his own veterinary surgeon, Chris Strong, to examine the horse. Chris knew Tim quite well as he had always seen to his horses for him, and as he had seen him competing around the shows he knew what sort of horse would be suitable.

On arrival at the seller's yard Chris got an uneasy feeling. The horse was tied up in the box and there were traces of saddle marks on him, so he had obviously been ridden already. He asked for the horse to be untied, and went in to examine him. While the horse seemed healthy, he did appear to be very quiet. Chris carried out all the routine procedures and took a blood sample for analysis if required. He found a few little knocks on the horse and discovered a couple of past injuries, but nothing that would make him advise against purchase. However, he was not happy about the 'boxy' appearance of the horse's feet, although it was perfectly sound. He thanked the seller and left the yard.

That evening Tim called and Chris told him of his findings. He said he would advise the analysis of the blood sample and to have the horse's feet X-rayed. Tim reluctantly agreed to this. The next day Chris telephoned to tell Tim that the blood sample had shown evidence of pain-killing drugs; Chris was suspicious of a cover-up, thinking the horse perhaps had navicular disease. Tim called the sellers and put this to them, and they told him the horse was no longer for sale. Tim was annoyed that he had lost out on what he had thought to be a good horse, but was thankful that he had listened to his veterinary surgeon who had prevented him from buying a totally unsound horse.

MORAL *Before you make your purchase always have a horse vetted by an experienced horse vet who will be looking for any cover-ups.*

6
LAWS AND LIABILITIES

THE NEXT STEP

Once the vet has approved the purchase of the horse, whether at a private or public sale, his task is completed. It is now up to you to arrange payment, or to haggle with the seller if the vetting has shown up something which, in your opinion, devalues the horse, even though it may still be suitable for you. It is not unreasonable to barter with the seller if the horse has a condition which affects its resale value. Having arrived at a price that is acceptable to both parties, you then need to discuss the points of any warranty.

If you are buying through an auction or sale, you must be fully aware of the organiser's 'conditions of sale' which will be printed in the sales catalogue, on display at the premises, or available on request. Conditions of sale differ from company to company, depending on the type of horses being sold. Often the conditions of sale can have more wide-ranging implications for the seller than for the buyer, and these are discussed in Chapter 8. As the buyer, however, there are certain points of which you should be fully aware.

There are no specific laws relating to buying and selling horses in the USA; existing consumer law applies.

A six-year-old Welsh Section B – or so it is advertised! You should be able to tell, but if it turned out to be twelve years old and a part-bred, you would be quite within your rights to be more than a little annoyed!

CONDITIONS OF SALE

Description

Whether buying privately, from a dealer, or through a sale, it is the responsibility of the seller to give an accurate description of the horse. However, you should do all you can to ensure that the horse is as described. Depending upon your knowledge, you will find some points of description easier to understand than others. For instance, even with only a basic knowledge of horses, you will be able to tell whether the colour of the horse, its approximate height and sex are as stated. A little more knowledge might help you to accept that the horse's breed and age are correct. A good knowledge of horses will enable you to tell whether statements such as 'good conformation' and 'clean legs' are correct. If, with the level of knowledge you have, you bought a horse believing the description given was correct, and you subsequently find it to be false, you may have cause to return the horse.

Some points may be trivial and may have occurred due to a typing error, or suchlike. Others may be quite critical. For instance, you would be quite within your rights to be more than a little annoyed if your six-year-old gelding turned out to be twelve.

Responsibility

This relates to who is accountable for the horse at what time. Generally, the seller is responsible for the horse until the money for its purchase has changed hands, when the responsibility falls to you, the buyer. However, there may be a period of overlap in between money changing hands and the horse being collected or delivered. The easiest solution is to make sure the horse is insured so that, in case of accident, liability falls to the insurance company, not the buyer or seller. However, while it may sound simple, this arrangement inevitably raises the question of who pays the insurance premium for this transitional period. The fairest way is for the seller to pay should the horse remain in his/her hands (perhaps while awaiting one of the specialist procedures of the pre-purchase examination as described on pages 108-110), and the buyer to pay while the horse is in his/her hands, perhaps on a trial period. Failing this agreement, both parties might compromise and pay half each until the purchase money is paid and the horse is safely delivered to the new owner, however long this should take.

Don't let the vendor get away with telling you that the papers belonging to the horse you have purchased will follow in the post. If you've paid your money, there should be no reason why you cannot take them with you

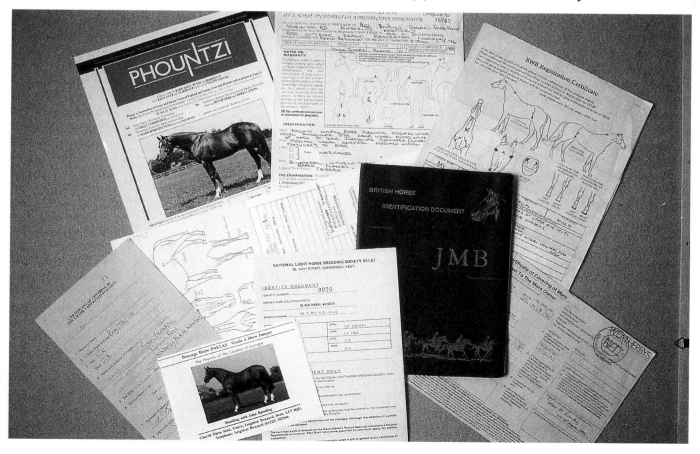

Vices

It is up to the seller to declare all known vices at the time of first viewing. (A description of vices and their complications is given on pages 65–82.) It is also sensible for you, the buyer, to ensure that you know exactly which vices are unacceptable to you, and to ask quite positively whether the horse is free from these. There may be cases where the seller is unaware of some obscure vice, but generally, anyone selling a horse will know it has had it for some time, or if a dealer, will be experienced enough to discover any vices a new horse on the yard might have. Should you detect that the horse has a vice about which you were not informed, you are within your rights to return it within a specified period: this will either have been set by the sales company or stipulated in the Sale of Goods Acts.

Returns

Generally, you can return a horse should anything become apparent that does not comply with the written warranty. Furthermore, verbal agreements do carry some weight, although if there are no witnesses it is, of course, simply your word against the seller's. It is therefore in your best interests to get a written warranty, detailing anything which you would find totally unacceptable in a horse and which the seller has confirmed not to be a problem in the horse you are buying. If you buy through an auction there will be certain conditions that render the horse returnable if the seller did not declare them. Each sale has its own set of specific conditions, but in general, the following apply for return:

- No papers – this applies if the horse is sold 'with papers', but then none materialise.
- Vices – most main vices, such as weaving, crib-biting, windsucking and box-walking, are covered.
- Wind operations on roarers or whistlers – such horses have abnormalities that make them 'make a noise', or they have been operated on to prevent its detection.
- A rig – a horse that behaves as though he is a stallion, even though he has been gelded (this may be as a result of improper gelding).
- Racing conditions – these apply to Thoroughbred racehorse sales and include various conditions such as non-registration.
- Declared ability – where a horse just does not have the ability he is stated to have. For instance a 'potential top show jumper' must be able to jump with ease.

- Declared temperament – a horse sold with a good temperament must be well mannered, easy to do and all in all a pleasure to own.
- In-foal brood mare – a mare that is sold in foal should be accompanied by a covering certificate from the stallion owner and a pregnancy certificate from the examining vet. In the absence of either of these, a vet must be called in to re-examine the mare. If she is not in foal, or the covering certificate does not materialise, then she is returnable.

In the USA horses are often 'sold as seen' without written warranties or evidence of suitability. However, many USA auctions do insist on the following declarations:

- that the horse had no impairment of vision;
- that it has not been de-nerved;
- that it does not crib-bite;
- that it is not a wobbler – a condition seen mostly in young horses of between three months and three years of age, when they experience increasing difficulty in co-ordinating themselves;
- that no racing restrictions apply, where appropriate;
- certain veterinary conditions stipulated by each sales company.

WARRANTIES

It is up to you, the buyer, to protect your own interests when buying a horse, and the old rule of *caveat emptor* (let the buyer beware) still holds strong. The buyer who bears in mind that many sellers exaggerate the good and forget to mention the bad is the one most likely to purchase a suitable horse. That is not to say that you should never consider an unwarranted horse, simply that if you do, you should consider the price you pay accordingly. Few sellers will offer a warranty unless asked for one, as there is always the fear of being sued, even if they are quite genuine. It is therefore up to you to ask for a warranty, and to have positive answers to your queries noted.

In law it is your responsibility to satisfy yourself about all attainable information. If it is there for you to see, you should have seen it (or the vet or the adviser working on your behalf should have done so), and the seller has no obligation to point out every lump and bump. For instance, if the horse clearly has a bowed tendon, it is up to you to spot it. If you bought the horse, you could not then return it because the seller did not tell you about the tendon. However, it is up to the seller to inform you of things that are not visible, but of which he or she is aware; for instance that the horse comes at you with its teeth bared if you enter its stable. Should any seller withhold such information, they are likely to be found blameworthy.

The warranty should be written in clear, easy-to-understand language. While you and the seller may be able to interpret horsy 'jargon', a judge may not be able to do so in the event of a dispute. The two main elements to be included in a warranty are:

- that the horse is sound in limb, wind and sight;
- that it is free from vice. If you are buying a horse with the knowledge of a certain vice, have this written in as an exclusion, so that other vices are still included in the warranty.

Covering certificate and breed registration document

Further to these points, which should be essential to every purchase, you may like to ask for the warranty to include:

- the horse's age;
- its ability;
- that it is good in traffic, to clip, to show, to box, to tie up;
- if applicable, that it is registered with a given society;
- its winnings, if any;
- its temperament;
- anything that you have enquired about and have been given a positive response to.

Should the seller have given you positive verbal information on these points, only to be reluctant to verify them in writing, you should begin to worry. Also ensure that only *true* facts are included in the warranty. For example, statements such as 'potential eventer', or 'believed sound' are useless: either the horse *has* evented, or it *is* sound. The seller will want to include any exclusions that he or she has informed you about. For example, he may want to put that this horse is known to weave, or to box-walk. The time limit for return must also be stipulated. Seven days is a reasonable figure for a general, straight purchase. However, you may wish to try to extend this if you are buying the horse but have agreed with the seller (usually a dealer in this case) that you may return it if it does not perform as requested. For instance, being good in traffic may be very important to you because you live on a main road. However, if the seller lives in a rural area, you cannot give the horse a fair trial. The seller may agree in such a case that you may return the horse if it proves to be frightened of the volume of traffic you intend to expose it to. In order to give this horse a fair trial, you will have to allow it to settle down in its new home and you may want to ride it in the fields or in a school for the first few days until you get used to it. By this time, seven days may have passed and your warranty period may be up without your having been able to give the horse a proper trial.

Once you are satisfied with the content of the warranty, you should decide upon method and time of payment, whether this is cash on collection, a deposit subject to a trial and so on. You should then have the seller sign it, and sign it yourself and have an independent person witness it.

It is not often that sellers in the USA offer a warranty.

TRICKS OF THE TRADE

Unfortunately, not everyone who sells a horse is honest. However, it would also be true to say that not everyone who buys a horse is honest either. The best policy, when buying a horse, it to treat everyone with a degree of caution, even if the seller genuinely seems to have your best interests at heart. Often the facts get stretched, and a horse that jumps nicely around an unaffiliated novice course is soon 'capable of jumping Foxhunters with ease'. Likewise, a horse that has hacked out a few times becomes a 'bombproof schoolmaster' overnight. Similarly, the novice rider who has had six lessons is suddenly on the shortlist for the Olympics – and so it goes on. Whether buyer or seller, everyone is out to impress. Therefore, as already stated, your best bet is to be totally honest with yourself about your abilities, and to satisfy yourself that this is the right horse for you without relying on the seller's word for it.

If you have never owned a horse before, how do you know when someone is trying to 'take you for a ride'? Obviously your adviser will be able to offer some advice, as will your vet, but there are a few tricks of the trade that you can look out for in order to avoid any buying pitfalls.

■ On arrival at the yard, do not allow the seller to tie the horse up in the box immediately, because this can be a way of hiding such traits as biting, barging, crib-biting and weaving. Ask politely for the horse to be left free for ten minutes or so, while you ask the seller any questions you have.

■ Do not allow the seller to keep talking without letting you get a word in edgeways. This is a way of stopping you from asking any awkward questions. In order to prevent the seller from doing this, come prepared with a written list of questions, and simply say, 'I would like to ask you these questions, and fire them off, waiting each time for an answer.

■ Feel the horse to ensure that it is not hot, and check for recent sweat marks around the girth area. These may indicate that the horse has been worked hard before your arrival. Perhaps to calm it down?

■ Look for signs of sedation or the horse's water being withheld. This is sometimes done in order to subdue a horse before a trial. Visible signs that should alert your suspicion might include lethargy, drowsiness, slow to blink if you flick your fingers near its eyes, and drooping head and neck. If you are suspicious, check to see if the horse has water. If not, ask for it to be offered some before the trial commences. Should it drink thirstily, you can be sure of foul play.

■ Take a good look at the horse's environment. Does its stable have a weaving grille, are its rugs torn, is its bed trampled in a circle, is it on a dust-free bedding and so on. Ask about anything you are not sure of.

■ When the horse is tacked up, take note of its bridle and saddle. What bit does it wear? Is it a strong one? If so, ask why. Does its saddle have a thick numnah (saddle pad) under it, or a thick gel pad? If so, ask why.

■ Does the seller tie the horse up before tightening the girth? If so, ask why. Does the horse object, perhaps by trying to bite?

■ When riding the horse, ask the seller for permission to put the horse through any trial that will help you to determine its suitability for your purposes. Should the seller object to any activities, ask why.

■ Do not be fobbed off with excuses such as, 'Well, it is really his day off', or 'I don't believe in riding horses on the roads because I have heard it can cause navicular.'

When your horse is returned to its box, ask if you can see it loose once more, but try to prevent the seller from feeding it immediately because this may prevent it from showing any vice

Should the seller object to any ridden activities, such as hacking out, you should insist that he/she gives you a reason for the objection

- Do not be soft-talked with phrases such as, 'I'm really sorry to see him go' (this may genuinely be the case, but now is not the time for sentiment on your part).

- Remember that 'dishonest sellers' can appear to be incredibly trustworthy.

- Finally, do not agree to give the seller first refusal to buy the horse back. This can prove to be a millstone around your neck and it is better for all concerned if all ties with the horse are severed cleanly.

If the seller leaves the horse's tack over the door, ask him to remove it because this is a good trick to prevent a weaver/crib-biter/windsucker showing his habit

- Do not be fooled with excuses such as, 'Sorry, he seems a bit "footy". The farrier only shod him yesterday, and he put the nails too high.'

- On return to the stable, ask to see the horse loose in its box once more. Do not allow the seller to feed it immediately or turn it out, as these actions can prevent it from showing any vices.

- If the seller leaves the saddle over the door, ask them to remove it. This is a good way to prevent a weaver showing its habit.

- Do not be badgered into making a quick decision by statements such as, 'You'll have to make your mind up quick as I've got another couple of people coming today', or 'With a jump like that he'll soon be snapped up.'

IDENTIFICATION

It always helps if the horse you are buying is accompanied by some form of official identification, such as a passport, breed registration document or freeze-marking document. This offers proof of correct identity, as nothing else can. Any horse's written identity starts with an identification diagram filled out by a vet who will record all markings, drawing them exactly as they appear on the horse, and including all distinguishing marks such as whorls, scars or odd colouring. This will ensure that the document relates exactly to the horse in front of the vet, so that no 'shady dealing' or swapping of papers can be achieved by less-than-honest sellers.

In years gone by, horses were rarely registered, or if they were, the papers usually got lost along the way, so it was quite common to buy a horse simply 'as seen' without any written documentation as to its breeding or age. Nowadays the situation is quite different in that most breeders register their stock with either their particular breed society or a national horse register; it is now therefore quite unusual to buy a horse without papers, unless they have been deliberately lost along the way. The reasons for this include:

- selling the horse as younger than it really is;
- allowing a successful horse to compete at lower levels with a different identity;
- trying to hide something that would go against the horse if known.

The horse may have lost its papers two or three owners ago, so the person selling to you may be perfectly genuine. However, once these are lost, a horse cannot be registered without total proof of age and identity. If you are told that the horse has papers, even if they are simply the horse's vaccination records, insist on seeing them at the time you view the horse. Promises to send them on are often never kept.

Once you have been handed the horse's documents, check them against the horse to ensure that they do relate to the animal you are buying. If you are

CERTIFICATE OF VETERINARY EXAMINATION OF A HORSE ON BEHALF OF A PROSPECTIVE PURCHASER

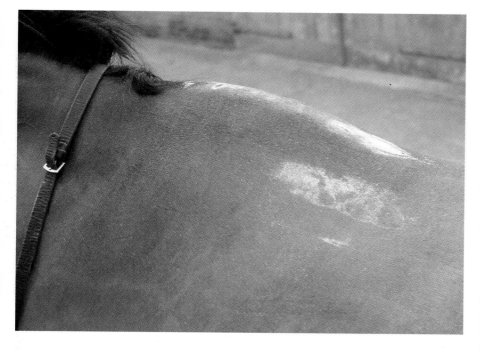

doubtful about anything you see, inform the seller that you would like the records to be made available to the vet during the pre-purchase examination. The vet can then double check anything that seems suspicious. Do remember, however, that apart from Thoroughbred passports and breed registration documents, many papers contain information supplied by the owner, so they are no guarantee of age. Such documents include vaccination and freezemarking certificates. It is surprising how often, after the age of eight, many horses' ages stand still. Without documentary proof of age it is quite common for a horse to be ten or twelve for at least five years!

In the USA the situation is quite different in that it is not common for there to be written evidence of past history. It would, however, be possible to get show records from the American Horse Shows Association, or race records in the case of Thoroughbreds.

A horse's written identity (left) will include details of all distinguishing marks including acquired marks such as old saddle sores (above)

AND FOR YOUR PART

Timewasters are a real nuisance when selling a horse, so make sure you are not considered to be one of them! Follow these simple guidelines to make buying a horse as stress-free as possible for both you and the seller.

- If you make an appointment to view a horse, ensure that you keep it and arrive on time, or else let the seller know in advance if you are going to have to alter the viewing time.

- Take only your adviser with you, not a lot of 'onlookers' hoping for a free ride.

- Only proceed to riding the horse if you really like what you see and are

seriously considering buying, provided the horse's ride, manners and so on turn out to be as desired.

- If you terminate the viewing due to unsuitability, do thank the seller for his/her time.

- If you feel the horse is more than you can afford, there is nothing wrong in haggling with the seller about price. However, if they will not lower it, do not start to get aggressive, or tell them that they are asking too much. Simply say the horse's price is out of your league. You must remember that you established the price (or should have) before viewing. And if the horse was far in excess of your

budget, you should never have gone to look at it.

- Never insult the seller simply because you are not getting the 'deal' you want.

- Some sellers are extremely honest and do care very much about their horses, especially youngsters which have been home-bred; they wish to sell to the right person, not just to a buyer with the right money. If you have been less than honest about your riding ability, then do not be surprised if such a seller refuses to sell you a horse because he or she considers that it is beyond your capabilities.

LEAVE NOTHING TO CHANCE

Heather Robinson bought a mare from a dealer who had been recommended to her by a showjumping friend. She viewed the horse and told the dealer her exact requirements: a safe, willing hack for her and her ten-year-old daughter. On trial the mare behaved very well both in the school and in traffic. She was vetted and Heather took possession of her three days later. The dealer gave a bill of sale that said the mare had been tried and approved, and that she was free from vice.

The day after she got the mare – Granite – home she discovered she tried to bite whenever being groomed; not just a little nip, but a really vicious lunge with all teeth bared. Heather thought perhaps she needed to settle in, so she allowed for this behaviour for the first few days, but it continued and got worse, extending to feed times and when she was tacked up.

Heather asked her vet to check the mare and he found nothing physically wrong. He did say that in his opinion Granite must have been a confirmed biter for some time, and that the dealer had obviously known how to cover it up at the time of vetting.

Heather called the dealer and asked if he would either refund the money or exchange the horse. He agreed to do the latter, but never came back to her, despite her numerous telephone calls. Heather then called him very early one morning and told him that if he did not come and collect the horse and refund her money she would take him to court. He told her to do just that.

Heather consulted a solicitor who told her she had a very good case. She had informed the dealer of her exact needs and the horse sold to her did not match these, so he could be found liable under the Sale of Goods Act. Also the horse had been sold free from vice, with a written statement to this effect, which it clearly proved not to be. Heather proceeded with court action. First she wrote to the dealer by recorded delivery and informed him that if her money was not returned within fourteen days she would be taking him to court. She heard nothing.

She asked her veterinary surgeon to give evidence in court on her behalf which he willingly did. The judge ruled in her favour and she was awarded the purchase price plus costs and interests.

She now has a perfectly suitable horse.

MORAL *Always inform the seller of your exact requirements and get a written warranty on any point that is important to you.*

7
BRINGING YOUR HORSE HOME

THE HORSE'S ROUTINE

The moment has come; you have had the horse examined and paid your money – it is now yours. Now is the time to think about taking it home and settling it into its new quarters. You are about to embark upon a learning process together. Undoubtedly *you* will have to get to know it, but in fact the horse has the more difficult task, for it will have to get to know not only you, but its new environment and companions as well. Problems relating to unsuitability can sometimes be avoided by recognising that a sudden change in a horse's routine and environment can affect its behaviour until it becomes accustomed to the new situation.

You will also have to allow enough time for a trusting relationship to develop with your horse, and there are no set limits as to how long this will take. Some horses settle in in a few hours, others can take days and possibly weeks. Patience is the key; however, there are a few things you can do to help the transition from one owner to another. First, check the following points with the seller:

- Is the horse kept mostly in a stable, or out in a field, or in at night and out during the day? If you change a field-kept horse's routine to mainly keeping it in, you may cause it to develop vices, or to become excitable and frisky due to the abrupt restriction to its accustomed exercise. A stable-kept horse does not seem to suffer problems when allowed more time at grass, however.

- Is the horse usually grazed with other horses, or on its own? If with other horses, is it usually timid or dominant?

- What does the horse normally get fed? A sudden change of diet could very well cause problems such as colic or overexcitability. Specifically ask how much (in pounds or kilograms) and what types of feed the horse gets, and how regularly; is it a good eater or are there certain foods it dislikes; does it normally receive any supplements; what sort of feeding bin does it eat out of; does it have ordinary hay or a dust-free alternative, and is its hay normally soaked? While you may decide to alter the horse's rations, this is something to be done gradually over a period of weeks, not the instant it arrives at your home.

- What is the horse's normal workload? If you suddenly over- or underwork it, its behaviour may change quite considerably. Again, the workload should be altered gradually. Also ask whether it is used to being ridden out alone or in company.

- What is its normal tack? Ride it in this until such time as you feel it warrants a change. The previous owner may have had its tack requirements finely tuned to what suits it best, in which case it would be pointless to change. Also ask if it wears any leg protection, and whether it is used to spurs and a whip, or not.

- When was the horse last wormed/shod/vaccinated? Plan your healthcare routine upon the information you receive; although you should always worm a horse on arrival at a new yard, and keep it off a grazing paddock for 48 hours afterwards. It is a good idea to book the farrier in plenty of time, giving at least two weeks' notice.

- Ask the seller if the horse has any particular likes or dislikes that you can cater for in order to ease it into its new situation.

Before your new horse's arrival you should have everything ready for it. If it is to be put into a stable, have a nice, thick bed ready, with plenty of hay and fresh water. Do not put a feed in its manger straightaway, as it may be hot after its journey. Check that there are no dangerous protrusions in the box, as a new horse is likely to walk around it quite a lot on first arrival. Check the field for any dangerous items such as loose fencing or discarded rubbish.

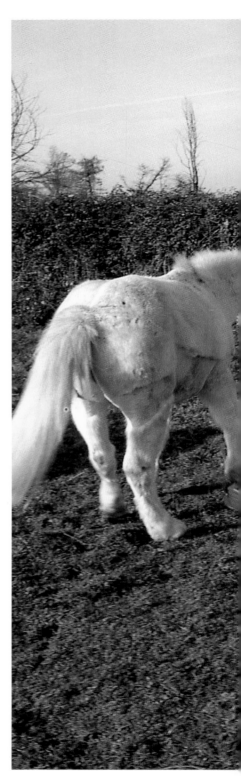

A group of horses running together in a field will have established a certain pecking order, and may well behave aggressively towards a stranger suddenly turned out with them. So work out a way of introducing your horse to the group by degrees, first letting them sniff and touch each other over the gate or fence, then turning him out in another paddock with just one, then another in turn until he has met the whole group

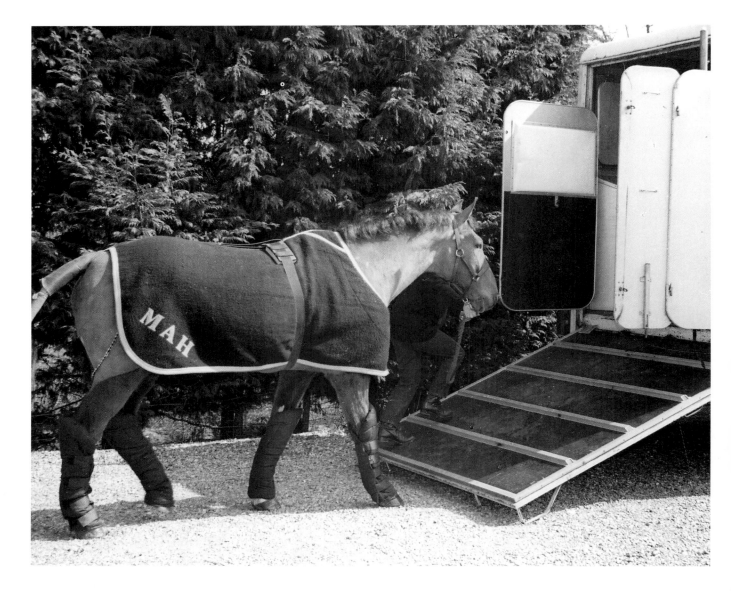

When collecting your new horse, remember to take travelling boots and any other protective items such as a tail bandage or tail guard. He might also need a rug, depending on the time of year

TRANSPORTING YOUR HORSE

Once everything is ready to receive your horse, you can set off to collect it, unless of course it is going to be delivered. Remember to take travelling boots, possibly a rug, a tail bandage or guard and a headcollar (halter) with you, as well as a haynet in the box. You may also need to take along a travelling companion for it if it is not used to travelling alone or is a youngster.

On arrival at the yard, check to ensure that the horse has no injuries or obvious illness. If it has, do not take charge of it but insist on the seller calling in a vet to offer an opinion. If all is well, deal with any necessary paperwork as discussed in the preceding chapters, and dress your horse ready for travelling. Make sure you have all its documentation and the warranty if there is one, and then load it up. Once loaded, get on your way as quickly as possible. Horses can become agitated if kept standing in a closed, motionless horsebox. Once moving, however, they seem to settle.

IMPORTING A HORSE

If you have bought a horse from overseas, you are obviously faced with the dilemma of getting it home safe and sound. When importing a horse there are three things you need to consider: the mode of transport, health, and quarantine or paperwork. The easiest way to import a horse is to have a reputable bloodstock agent or horse transportation firm take care of it for you. They will arrange all the details, such as health certificates, examinations, blood tests, quarantine and grooms to accompany the horse while travelling. All you will have to do is to inform them where they should pick the horse up from and where to deliver it, and of course, to pay them for doing so. Because there is so much to think about when importing a horse, and because regulations change so rapidly, this really is a sensible way to organise things, even if it does appear to be costly.

If you decide to import the horse yourself, you can, within Europe, do so by air, sea or road. Long-haul transatlantic journeys will obviously involve flying. For full details of import regulations and conditions in the UK you should contact the Ministry for Agriculture, Fisheries and Food (Animal Health International Trade Division) at Government Buildings (Toby Jug Site), Hook Rise South, Tolworth, Surbiton, Surrey KT6 7NF. However, if you intend to take your own horsebox and bring your horse back yourself, the following points may be of some guidance:

- Your lorry must be totally reliable.
- Carry spare parts.
- Carry both human and equine first-aid kits, both for your own protection and because they are a legal requirement in many European countries.

- Have breakdown and roadside recovery insurance.
- Obtain (from the Department of Transport) a road permit, and (from your own insurance company) a green card for the countries through which you will be travelling.
- Study the countries that you will be driving through. In particular, take note of their road signs and the side of the road they drive on.
- Check on road tolls, and make sure you have enough money in the right currency with you.
- Check on ferry availability and times.
- Take another experienced horse person and box driver with you.
- Ensure that you can communicate with local people by learning important phrases that will help you to find

Importing a horse entails a great deal of complicated documentation, and the easiest way to do it is to arrange for a reputable agent or firm to take care of all the details for you. Regulations change rapidly and the agents have a lot of experience in all the legal and practical aspects of travel

Obviously seasoned travellers! The loading procedure into the aircraft is so quick and efficient that the horses are caused a minimum of stress and anxiety: it obviously hasn't bothered these two in the least

a vet, stabling or food, and take phrase books along with you. If you get in a muddle, copy what you want to say onto a piece of paper and ask the person with whom you are speaking to read it.

- Be aware of lairage restrictions. These are requirements for unloading and resting your horse, usually for a minimum of ten hours on long journeys. A veterinary surgeon will be appointed to check your horse over before you will be allowed to continue your journey, so double check your times for connections and make sure you have allowed plenty of leeway.
- Carry your own water, but remember that the horse will be used to the water it has been drinking, so fill its water containers before you leave its yard.

- Make sure your horsebox will lock securely.
- Make sure that your horse is insured for the journey.

Horse importation into the USA is a complicated business, and regulations depend on the country of origin. For full details contact the United States Department of Agriculture, Riverdale, Maryland.

Air travel

Air travel is not common in the case of everyday or competition horses. However, racehorses are travelled in this way quite

frequently. Flights to and from America run about two to three times a month in the autumn, thus coinciding with the bloodstock sales, while flights to Australia run only once every three to six months.

Before boarding a plane, the horse's hind shoes will have to be removed. It will not require rugs for warmth as temperatures are controlled; however, it will need the normal travelling protection of boots, tail guard and perhaps poll guard. Horses can either be flown as 'cargo' on scheduled flights, or on chartered planes. They are either put onto 'partitioned' pallets and then manoeuvred into the plane by means of a hoist, or are led up a ramp into stalls specially designed for the purpose.

INTRODUCING YOUR HORSE TO ITS NEW HOME

The first thing to do when your horse is in its stable is to go away and give it some peace. Obviously you will want to observe it for a while, but you can do this virtually unnoticed, or at least without popping into its box every couple of minutes. The horse will want to explore its new accommodation and get used to the new sights, sounds and smells. On no account should you have a welcoming party on hand for its arrival, because it will only upset it to have lots of people looking at it and talking around it. Nor is it a good idea to turn a new horse straight out into a field as it may gallop wildly about, calling and looking for a way out. Bring your new horse home in the morning to give it plenty of time to settle down in daylight before being shut in a strange box for the night.

Whenever you approach the horse, make sure it can see and hear you. Talk to it and lay a firm hand on it when you ask it to move over. From the start you must insist on good manners: on no account should you tolerate biting, kicking, bolshiness or plain bad manners of any sort. This is not settling in, this is the horse trying it on to see how much it can take advantage of you. Let it know

that it cannot get away with such behaviour. Use your voice to warn it, but if this seems ineffective, give it a short, sharp smack. It is vital that you set the ground rules from day one. If your horse gets the better of you at this time, you will have an uphill struggle to retain its respect in the future, which is a great pity as it will detract from any happy association that you may have with it.

Once the horse is settled, you will probably want to turn it out into the field. This can be a worrying time, as a new horse is bound to run around and squeal at the others. If you can do so, it will pay to turn it out with just one other quiet horse first of all. Introduce them first. Obviously you will want to keep a close eye on the newcomer at this time, but rest assured that no matter how much galloping, bucking and squealing your new one indulges in, it will probably settle down after half an hour or

so. Meanwhile you, on the other hand, may have bitten your nails right down to the quick! If other horses are to join the two in the field, introduce them one by one and let the group settle. New horses can get 'ganged up on' so be careful if your new horse is either a very timid or very dominant type.

When you start to ride your horse, keep its work fairly undemanding for the first week. Ride it in a manège initially to ensure that it is still the sensible horse that you tried, but do bear in mind that you will both be a little apprehensive. Find someone quiet to hack out with on your first few outings, and you will soon establish a routine that suits you both. Providing you are fair with your horse, praising it when it is good and punishing it when it does wrong, it will soon come to learn what is expected of it, and a relationship founded on trust will grow and blossom into a happy experience for both of you.

At first you may want to turn your horse out on his own until he has settled into his new environment, though if he is obviously fretting for company it would probably be as well to turn out a quiet horse with him; some horses if left all alone will try to jump out in their search for a friend. Then introduce any further companions one by one over the next few days

THEFT PREVENTION

Security and theft prevention have become important responsibilities for every horse-owner. Having found your ideal horse, the last thing you want is to lose it overnight through a lack of security. There are many security methods available, from freezemarking to hoof branding, but it can be difficult to decide which is most suitable for your circumstances. Obviously, if every horse were freezemarked, horse theft could be wiped out. The problem is that many people are against freezemarking for one reason or another – and of course, there is always that element of 'It'll never happen to me'.

Freezemarking puts a permanent brand on the horse's back, which does deter thieves and makes the horse immediately recognisable for return if stolen. Freezemarked horses are often dumped once the thief realises that the horse is marked. If your horse is rugged, so hiding the mark, it is a good idea to paint the mark on the outside of the rug in big lettering as this may also deter a thief because it informs him what is hidden underneath the rug. If you are worried about show judges putting horses down the order because of freezemarks, don't be. No respectable judge would give a freezemark any consideration when assessing a horse's conformation or outline. In the UK, no respectable

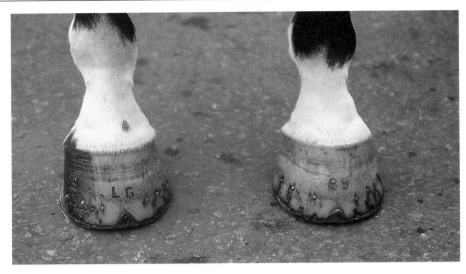

Hoof-branding is a visible deterrent, although unlike freezemarking it will have to be repeated as the brand grows down the hoof

slaughter-house will accept a horse that is freezemarked without its papers. This is an added deterrent to thieves who steal horses for meat.

If you find freezemarking unacceptable, other methods include hoof branding and identichipping. Hoof branding provides another visible deterrent, although not a permanent one. The hooves are branded, usually with your post code, the procedure needing to be repeated as the brand grows down.

Identichipping is when a microchip is implanted into the horse's neck. This can then be read with a scanner for identification of a particular horse. Such a system does not provide a visible deterrent and so will not prevent theft, but it will help to identify a horse as yours should it be recovered after having been stolen.

When choosing a security system you should note the following points:

- The company should have a 24-hour back-up service so that a horse's details can be checked without delay.
- It should take action in order to recover your horse if it becomes aware it has been stolen.
- The company should offer a nationwide service.
- It should have good relations with the police force, offering immediate access to them when required.
- It should be in regular and familiar contact with the police force, with abattoirs, port authorities, and also sale organisers, local horsewatch schemes and veterinary surgeons.

In order to make identification of your horse as easy as possible, you should fill out a description chart and take photographs of your horse in both summer and winter, from both sides and from front and rear.

Freezemarking puts a permanent brand on the horse's back, which deters thieves and makes the horse easily recognisable for return if stolen

UNSUITABLE PURCHASES

It is not until you have had a horse at home for a while that you can truly decide whether it is totally suitable for your purpose or not. You may find that it does some things that are a little bit of a nuisance, but which on the whole can be lived with. However, what should you do if you find that you just do not get on with the horse?

The first thing to decide is:

- whether the problem is caused by a clash of personalities between you and the horse; or
- whether the horse is simply not as was described by the seller.

In both cases the first step is to contact the seller and explain the trouble you are having, aiming to reach an amicable agreement. If the horse fulfils its description but you simply have not 'clicked' with it, the seller is under no obligation to help you. However, if the horse is *not* as described, then you may have some redress in law if the seller is uncooperative. In this case try to discuss the following options: would he or she be prepared to:

- take the horse back and refund your money?
- exchange the horse for another, more suitable one?
- refund part of your money?

A private seller is unlikely to want to agree to any of these options as, obviously, he or she wanted the horse out of his/her hands in the first place. However, many dealers are more sympathetic and will often try to find an alternative horse for you. You are generally entitled to return a horse bought at auction if a problem arises which contravenes what the catalogue stated or what the auctioneer said verbally about

the horse, even though this was not mentioned in the catalogue. However, you should confirm at the time of purchase how many days you have in which to inform the auctioneers of misdescription or breach of warranty. You will have no redress if you return the horse outside any specified time limit.

Breach of warranty

Where the horse is simply unsuitable because you do not get on with it there is no breach of warranty. The horse is 'as you bought it' and your only course of action may be to sell it on to someone more compatible. However, if the horse is certainly not 'as described', you need

to contact an experienced equestrian solicitor who will advise on the likelihood of success in establishing liability. A breach of contract is considered in the light of whether a false statement is a major or minor one, and compensation will be awarded accordingly, if proven.

If your horse proves unsuitable it may also be that you can hold responsible the veterinary surgeon who carried out the pre-purchase examination if he:

- failed to detect a fault which undoubtedly must have been present at the time of the examination; or
- the horse had a permanent problem which must have been present at the time of examination.

Where a purchase proves unsuitable you must decide whether the problem is caused by a clash of personalities between you and the horse, or whether the horse is simply not as was described by the seller

In law, disputes between a buyer and a seller are classed as civil matters. As such, the matter is decided on a balance of probabilities, often coming down to whose evidence is more acceptable. If you bought your horse on the basis of what the seller told you, or what an advertisement said about the horse, and this subsequently turned out to be false, 'misrepresentation' arises. To bring a successful claim you will need to prove that the seller did not have grounds for believing that what he said was true. If you are successful in establishing misrepresentation, you will be entitled to a full refund or to compensation. However, establishing this can be difficult and you are strongly advised to engage an experienced equestrian solicitor if you feel you do have a valid case. Horses bought from a dealer in the UK (not a private sale) come under the Sale of Goods Act, which states that 'goods must be of merchantable quality and fit for the purpose for which they are sold'.

WARRANTED

The word 'warranted' on a contract of sale does not guarantee anything except the horse or pony's soundness, unless extra factors are stated afterwards.

INSURANCE

Ideally you should arrange insurance cover from the moment you become the legal owner of the horse. This will either be the moment you hand over your money, or the moment the hammer falls at a sale. Obviously, if you are buying from a private seller or a dealer you will have a few days in which to arrange cover before collection. However, you can never be sure if you will actually buy a horse at a sale, so how can cover be arranged in such circumstances? Many insurance companies will offer insurance cover from the 'fall of the hammer', but you must notify them of your intentions beforehand. This is a sensible idea. Remember that should the horse you have just bought get hurt between the sale ring and the horsebox, it is your problem.

When you come to insure the horse, it is most important that you have the receipt for the sum you paid for it. Should you buy a horse for £3,500 and you have a receipt to prove it, you will have no trouble in insuring the horse for this amount. Likewise you will also be paid the full £3,500 should your horse be killed in an accident, sustain injuries that prevent it from carrying out the job you bought it for, or have to be put down to prevent further suffering, providing you take out the correct cover.

What policy?

Riding and handling your horse with all due care and attention will help to cut down on many mishaps and injuries, but inevitably, accidents will happen. Similarly, while you may take all sensible precautions against theft or damage, you cannot be totally sure that your horse or belongings are 100 per cent safe. It is obvious, then, that insurance to cover the unforeseen is a sensible, if not essential, precaution. While having insurance is not yet a legal requirement of horse ownership, it should be just as important to a horse owner or rider as to a motorist. A horse represents a great investment to most people and should therefore be insured as quickly as possible after purchase.

Most companies offering horse insurance offer standard policies, with varying degrees of risk: the greater the risk involved, the higher the premium – the general riding horse will be cheaper to insure than the Advanced eventer, for example. However, if your requirements do not fall into a standard category, then you should enquire about a tailor-made policy to suit your purpose. Cover for the following eventualities is important to any horse and rider/driver:

VETERINARY FEES

Usually this will be up to a maximum price, depending on the policy and risk factor. You should make sure that the quoted cover is not limited to a percentage of the sum insured, but is that which you will receive per claim. You usually have to pay the first part (£75 in 1996) of any claim. If you would like your horse to receive complementary treatments such as hydrotherapy, physiotherapy or homoeopathy, you should check that your policy covers this.

PERSONAL ACCIDENT

This policy covers you, or any person riding/driving your horse with your permission, in the event of an accident. Some policies also offer cover for temporary total disablement, immediate hospital care or dental cover.

MORTALITY

This should cover full replacement value if the horse dies or has to be put down. Check whether or not the insurers require you to inform them before putting a horse down, as this can prolong unnecessary suffering. Some policies do not cover a horse under a general anaesthetic unless it is undergoing a life-saving operation, so you should find a policy which will.

THIRD PARTY LIABILITY

Lack of third party liability could prove very expensive, and so it is really essential to every person who keeps a horse. Damages soon add up. Just imagine if your horse got loose on the roads, ran into a person's garden, smashed their greenhouse, trampled their roses, stood on their dog – could your bank balance cover the bill without insurance?

SADDLERY AND TACK

Tack theft is increasing at an alarming rate so you should make sure it is covered by your policy for theft, and for damage too.

IMMEDIATE COVER

Some policies do not commence cover for 30 days, which is quite obviously unacceptable. If, however, you have a credit card it is possible to insure your horse from the moment of purchase (see page 132).

LOSS OF USE

This does not mean that the horse can no longer be used, but that it can no longer be used for the purpose it was bought for. For example, the horse might be saved from death by veterinary technology, but it might not be fit to resume a competitive life. It is important, therefore, to decide what you intend to use, and insure, your horse for. If it is only insured for light hacking and dressage and it then gets injured in a cross-country event, you will not be covered.

Selecting the right insurance company

To begin with, you might ask your vet which insurance company he would recommend. He will probably have filled in many forms relating to equestrian claims and so he should have a good idea about which ones are known to give a prompt and helpful service. A horse-owning friend or colleague or your riding school might be able to give a personal recommendation.

When considering insurance without a personal recommendation, it is a good idea to shop around as some insurers are more competitive than others, and some policies are fairer than others. The most expensive quote does not always mean you will get the best cover. However, it is silly to settle for a policy which does not meet all your requirements simply because you will save money on the premium. Realising that insurance is essential does not make it any easier to pay, however, so many insurance companies will now accept monthly or quarterly instalments which might ease the financial burden of horse ownership a little.

When choosing insurance, make a list of your needs and ensure that these are covered by the policy. Read all the small print, and if you are unsure on any point, call the company and ask to have it explained fully in easily understood terms. If you flick over the small print you might find when it comes to claiming that you are not covered because of a minor detail. In particular, check what exclusions there are for vet's fees, for public liability and for tack.

Horse insurance in the USA is similar to that in the UK. As with membership to the BHS, liability insurance is included in full AHSA membership.

Consider taking out a policy that covers you, or someone else riding your horse, for personal accident. For instance, this will help you to pay someone else to look after your horse if you are unable to do so

New horse ownership

It is a good idea to budget for insurance when considering horse ownership. Most policies cover a certain amount of veterinary fees, and you can choose whether you want to insure against loss of use and tack theft as well. There are various categories for the work you will be doing with your horse. Competing in hunter trialling obviously carries a higher injury risk than hacking, which is reflected in the premiums. As a rough guide, premiums will work out at about 10 per cent of your horse's value.

Cover for non-owners or riders

A common misconception is that most horse-related injuries are the result of falls. In fact you are just as likely to incur an injury off a horse as on one. Common injuries result from bites, kicks, being squashed against the stable wall, and being stood on. It makes sense, then, to have a policy which covers injuries experienced while handling the horse, as well as when riding or driving. Also, if you ride someone else's horse which they have insured, make sure that you are covered for public liability. Many insurers will cover an additional named rider aged between five and sixty-five, quite cheaply.

The horse at home

Third party liability or personal insurance will cover you against possible claims arising from any damage your horse does to people or property, or from disease or accidental injury. When considering insurance you should find a policy that will cover you against straying and accidental trespass; for example, when a horse gets out of its field. All policies are subject to specific terms, conditions and exceptions, so if you are not sure about the conditions, ask the insurance company to explain them before paying any premium. If you are only looking after or borrowing a horse, you should make sure that the horse's owner has the necessary insurance cover. This will ensure that you are protected if the horse causes any damage or injury should it escape from your field. In the UK, every fully paid-up member of the British Horse Society is covered for personal liability up to £2 million of cover for any one claim in respect of using a horse or a horse-drawn vehicle.

As many older horses are kept solely at grass, it is worth mentioning the influence age has on insurance. Some companies will only insure up to a maximum age of twelve, others go up to fifteen or sixteen, while a few will insure a horse up to twenty years of age. However, look very carefully at the policy because what is actually covered might not be worth paying the premium for. Up to twelve years of age the insurers will cover vets' fees for injury and accident or illness. However, once past twelve, some policies only cover for injury and accident, but not for illness, or some will limit the amount of cover per claim; so check this out if you have an older horse.

The stabled horse

When taking out insurance you should inform your insurers where your horse is to be kept and whether it is to be stabled or at grass. Stabled horses may attract a lesser premium as they are deemed to be more secure and at less risk of injury. However, if, having informed your insurers that you stable your horse every night, you then decide to keep it at grass, you should make this known to them. You should also inform your insurers if your horse is injured or ill and needs attention from a vet, whatever the problem. If your horse dies, or you claim for loss of use further to an injury or illness some time ago, you can expect some hassle from your insurers due to such late notification.

You are also expected to take all reasonable precautions to keep your horse in good health, including having it regularly vaccinated. If your horse gets tetanus from a cut because you failed to keep up with its vaccination boosters, your insurers may refuse to pay out.

Many horse policies now also include stable insurance. In the event that your horse's stable is totally destroyed by fire, you may receive a set fee per week to stable it somewhere else until a new stable can be built.

Insuring tack and equipment

Insuring your tack is also a sensible precaution and most policies cover it for fire damage, accidental damage, or theft (following forcible/violent entry to a locked, private building), on the same policy as your horse.

Insurance for beginners

All riding schools and training centres should be covered for negligence under their own insurance policy, and this will cover you if you get hurt due to their negligence. However, the policy will not cover an accident that was deemed to be plain bad luck. Therefore, in the interests of your own safety it is a good idea to think about protection for yourself, especially if you borrow a horse or if you ride regularly but don't own your own horse. A few companies offer rider-only cover or specially designed rider plans. While you can enhance your own personal safety by wearing the correct gear and being sensible while riding or attending to horses, you can never know what might happen. Remember, not all accidents can be prevented, so it pays to cover yourself.

If you are working or have family commitments you should also look into the possibility of covering yourself against loss of earnings or the need to pay for home help should you be injured. In addition, if you compete, in whatever field, you should have some sort of insurance policy for yourself. While the horse you are riding will probably be insured against accident and injury, you might not be. If the horse you are riding is not your own, check with the horse's owner to see whether you are covered. In any event it is a sensible idea to take out personal insurance which covers you when riding in competitions, whether on your own horse or not.

If you are not sure about anything to do with your insurance policy, always ring up the company and ask. And if you are still not sure, keep on asking until you are quite happy that you have completely understood exactly what it is you are paying for.

All riding schools and training centres should be covered for negligence under their own insurance policy; thus if you get hurt due to their negligence, *their* policy should reimburse you – *proving* them negligent may be quite another issue, however!

A HORSE IN THE GARDEN!

Richard Daley had wanted a horse of his own all his life and now, at the age of twenty-eight, was in a position to buy one. He had a very good job and a substantial amount of savings in the bank. However, he had a problem in that he could not find a decent livery yard in his area. He lived in a detached house, although his neighbours were fairly close, but did have room in his large garden for a stable and a small turn-out area. He could also rent grazing for more suitable turn-out across the road. He asked his neighbours whether they would mind a 'horse next door', and they said they would quite like it.

Richard then contacted his local authorities to find out whether he would need planning permission to erect a stable in the garden. They said that he did not need planning permission, but he would need to satisfy local building regulations. This he did and he also contacted the local environmental health officer for advice on the prevention of rats and mice and on the disposal of the muck heap. He was acutely aware that he could not afford to upset his neighbours, and kept them informed at every step. One of his neighbours offered to help and Richard was only too glad to involve him.

Having set up his stable and grazing properly, Richard then went in search of the 'perfect horse'. He took along his instructor and when he found one that seemed suitable, he had it vetted. All went well and Richard is now the proud owner of a horse 'in the garden'.

Whenever he is away his neighbours help to look after the horse and he has become something of a talking point along the street. People come to collect dung for their gardens and offers of carrot tops are always welcomed!

MORAL *If you always inform those around you of your intentions, you will make allies, not enemies. Owning a horse should be an enjoyable experience, not a battle.*

8
SELLING YOUR HORSE

REASONS FOR SELLING

Selling a much loved horse or pony can be quite a traumatic experience, especially if the horse has been a member of the family for many years. However, the process can be made less painful if certain procedures are followed. The most important consideration is to ensure that the horse finds the right sort of home, where it will be well looked after and not pushed beyond its limits.

There are many reasons for selling a horse. You may simply be giving up; you may have found that the horse is not really suitable for you; or you may have physically outgrown your horse or pony; your horse may be getting older and needing a quieter life; you may have outgrown your horse's ability; your personal circumstances may have changed, and so on. When you are a seller, you want everyone to believe your reasons for selling – because, of course, they are true. However, remember when you were the buyer and how suspicious you were of any reasons for sale. You should bear in mind that the people coming to look at your horse will be suspicious too, so you should do all you can to allay their fears.

Before you reach for a pen to write out your advertisement or complete a sales entry form, however, have you truly considered: (a) why you want to sell your horse; and (b) whether there are any other more suitable options? If you have to make enough money on your horse in order to buy another, there really is no option but to sell it on. If money is not the problem, but making room for another horse is, you might consider loaning your horse so that you can still have some contact with it. If you do decide to loan your horse (see pages 20–1), be sure to arrange a proper agreement with the loanee, and do not accept any money, however small, in payment because such a fee can be construed in law as a purchase fee. An outgrown pony can lead another life as a driving pony or as a companion for another horse, while your older mare might breed you a very nice foal. In this case, however, you should only consi-der breeding from your mare if she is of good conformation, sound and healthy, and only if you will have a use for the resulting foal, as breeding is certainly not a way of making a bit of money.

If your horse is old, or is becoming feeble, you should think very carefully about selling it on at all (see page 155). Such horses really deserve a quiet retirement in return for their loyal service to you. If you can no longer keep such a horse at home, you should look for a respectable retirement home; however, be sure that you inspect such a home and also contact veterinary surgeons and horsewatch schemes in that locality to see if they know of any problems with it. It is a sad fact that some very crafty and despicable people buy old horses for a pittance, saying they only want them as companions, and then sell them on as 'younger' animals for more money – so make doubly sure where your old horse is going.

WAYS OF SELLING

Having made the decision to sell your horse, what is the best way to go about it? The various options are:

- word of mouth;
- private sale;
- through a dealer;
- at an auction;
- through an agency.

By far the best way of selling any horse is by word of mouth because it ensures that your horse or pony will be going to someone who is connected to you in some way, perhaps a friend of a friend, a colleague at work, or another member of your Pony Club branch. This means that you will always know how your horse is doing without having to infringe on the new owner's privacy with the horse. Word-of-mouth sales often come out of chance conversations. You may be at a show, talking to friends, when you happen to say you are thinking of selling your horse. If the horse is well behaved and without any problems, before you know it you may get a call from someone you have never met saying, 'So-and-so told me your horse was for sale and he might be just what I am looking for'. Immediately you feel quite good about this because it means you will not have to advertise the horse and sell it into an unknown future. That your horse will suit this person is not guaranteed, of course, but it must be fairly suitable for your friends to have recommended it.

The more problems your horse has, of course, the less likelihood there is of selling it in this way, as its reputation will probably be well known. Selling ponies by word of mouth is extremely beneficial and is usually done quite extensively through the Pony Club. Good ponies are hard to find, especially for novice riders, so if a friend recommends one to you, be sure to go and look at it.

Private sale

More horses are sold privately in the UK and USA than by any other means. This is largely due to the fact that in this way the seller has complete control over who buys the horse and for how much. However, in order to let people know your horse is for sale, you will, of course, have to advertise it in some way. This is usually through a national magazine which carries quite an extensive 'horses for sale' section but, equally, could be done by putting advertisements

The most important consideration when selling a much loved horse or pony is to ensure it finds the right sort of home where it will be well looked after

in local papers or on your feed merchant's or saddler's notice boards. If you do advertise your horse, make sure that you will be around the telephone when the calls start to come in. It is amazing how many people put an advertisement in a paper only to go on holiday when it comes out. People who want to buy a horse want to do so immediately. If you are not in on the first call, they may call back, but more likely they will have gone on to the second horse on their list and may even have bought it before you start to answer your telephone.

- So **Rule one** is '*Be ready for your calls*'.

- **Rule two** is, '*Be prepared for the caller's questions*'. Even though you may have owned your horse for many years, when someone asks you something about it, you can rest assured that your mind will go completely blank. A pause on the telephone after a question is asked does nothing to instil any confidence in your would-be buyer, so have a list of all the horse's main details in front of you: age, height, breeding, colour, ability, experience, and so on. This list will also prove useful if someone telephones while you are out because another family member can then give the caller the basic details; and if they seem interested, they can take the number so that you can call them back upon your return.

- **Rule three** is, '*Be available*'. Having decided that they want to come and see the horse, a buyer will want to do

If you do advertise your horse, be sure you are near the telephone to receive the calls when they come in

so as soon as possible. If you cannot be available until next weekend, they will probably have bought another horse by then, so forward planning is essential.

- **Rule four** is, '*Be truthful*'. This was discussed in Chapter 7, but it is so important that it is worth mentioning again. There is nothing worse for a buyer than to have a horse described over the telephone only to find that it is nothing like that upon his arrival to view.

- **Rule five** is, '*Be friendly but businesslike*'. Welcome the customer and answer his questions as best you can, but try not to stand chatting all day. Remember rule one: other people may be trying to call you.

- **Rule six** is, '*Be fair to your horse; do not sell it to someone totally unsuitable*'.

WORDING AN ADVERTISEMENT

You should view your advertisement as your shop window. Unless it impresses the potential customer, nobody will bother to come in and buy, so it is crucial that you put all the relevant information about your horse in the most appealing way. Study these two advertisements and then decide which impresses you more.

THE SIX RULES FOR PRIVATE SALE

1. Be ready for your calls.
2. Be prepared for your caller's questions.
3. Be available.
4. Be truthful.
5. Be friendly but businesslike.
6. Be fair to your horse.

16.1hh, grey gelding,

10 years old, has jumped, done hunter trials. Good to clip, box shoe etc., nice temperament, good manners. £4,000
Tel: 01234 98765

Stunning

Grey gelding, by Potty. 10 years old, with plenty of experience.
Has been a consistent winner in showjumping and hunter trials.
Excellent temperament – a gentleman in every respect.
16.1hh ideal schoolmaster. £4,000   Please telephone 01234 98765

Both advertisements describe the same horse, but a little more thought has gone into the second advertisement. Of course you should not put statements such as 'stunning' unless your horse *does* have lovely looks, but if it does, then you should ensure that such details are not omitted from an advertisement. You would normally only advertise a horse once, so make sure you get it right first time. If you have to use more words, making the advertisement a little dearer, then so be it. Don't try to cut corners with your advertisement – it is your only means of letting potential buyers know that your horse is available, and that it is just what they want. It is debatable whether you should give details of the price or not. I am of the opinion that you should, as this is one of the first questions a buyer will ask. What is the point of having a caller ring up simply to be informed that your horse is out of his/her league? At least if you do stipulate a price you can be sure you only get calls from people who can afford the sort of money you are asking.

Half the battle is getting buyers to come and see *your* horse as opposed to another one advertised at the same time. They probably will go to see others, but if you word your advertisement cleverly, you may persuade them to come and see your horse first, and so those which they might have thought suitable will be at a disadvantage. No advertisement will sell a horse (although horses have been known to sell over the telephone, usually because of their breeding or some other knowledge which enables the potential buyer to know the horse is just what he is looking for) but if it gets the buyers into your yard, then it has done its job. Your horse will sell, or not sell, on his own merits, but one thing is for sure: if no buyers come to look at him, it doesn't matter whether he is the next Milton, Red Rum or King William.

You may want to include a photograph with your advertisement. If so, make sure that it is a side-on shot, and that the horse is standing up correctly

Dealers

If you simply cannot be bothered with all the hassle (and the rules of private sales will help you to decide this), then you can opt to send your horse away to a dealer who will sell it on your behalf. The benefits of this are that you will have none of the bother; the dealer will know the right price for your horse and will neither under- nor over-price it; and your horse can be tried where there are suitable facilities. The drawbacks are that you will have less control over who buys it, and you will have to pay the dealer for his/her service. Payment can be taken in two ways: either the dealer will expect a weekly fee for preparing your horse and showing it to potential customers; or he/she will expect a commission on the sale. Some dealers offer a split arrangement based on a half-price weekly fee with half the normal commission also.

One of the major benefits of selling through a dealer is that he will probably have many buyers coming into the yard and so your horse will have a better chance of being sold fairly quickly. However, you must be sure to go only to a recognised dealer, one who has a good reputation and has been in business for some time. Unfortunately there are dealers who will sell your horse for you, only to cheat you out of some of your money or keep you waiting a considerable time for it. Generally this is not the case, of course, and I would not wish to give respectable dealers a bad name; but you should be aware that there *are* a dishonest few, so ask around – ask your farrier, your vet, a friendly saddler or your feed merchant, as these people hear what is going on.

Most dealers will not object to the terms of sale between them and owners being put down in writing, so do this at the outset. If they seem cautious about doing this, then you should be cautious of them.

If your horse has been with a dealer for a number of weeks but without a successful sale, you should review the situation. Either your horse is too dear for what it really is, or the dealer is not a particularly successful one, in which case you will either have to take the horse away and try to sell it yourself, or

advertise it in a separate advertisement. (Most dealers take out an advertisement listing a number of horses for sale, or simply with wording such as: 'quality horses always for sale'.)

Whatever the arrangements you make with the dealer, ensure that you know how you will receive your money once the horse is sold. Ideally the cheque should be made out to you, and you should then pay the dealer's commission. However, many dealers have been caught in this way by owners not paying up, so the dealer may insist on having the payment made out to him so that he can stop his commission before payment to you. Either way, have the terms written into your agreement at the start.

Auctions

There are three main reasons for selling your horse through an auction: the first is to eliminate all the hassle of dealing with potential customers coming to view your horse; the second is to off-load a problem horse, which can be done in this way because, at auctions, the Sale of Goods Act does not apply; and the third reason is to sell a horse at a sale specifically designed for its type, which is of benefit to sellers because many genuine buyers attend for the convenience of seeing a number of suitable horses at one time. Such sales include Thoroughbred sales for racehorses in and out of training, and high performance sales for competition horses.

When entering a horse for a sale you must be careful about the description you give. Thus if you describe your horse as a showjumper, it must be capable of showjumping. However, this description does not imply that the horse is a good ride, or even good to handle. A hack must be well behaved when ridden, but this does not necessarily mean that it is quiet in traffic – the previous owner may never have taken the horse off his/her farm! A good mover simply implies that the horse does not hobble along on three legs, and so on. As the seller, you are relying on the ignorance of potential buyers, and it is up to the buyer to check out anything that is not stated. You are under no compulsion to state anything about your horse –

though obviously, the less information there is, the more suspicious the average buyer will be. Remember, the only way a buyer can return your horse is if it has been misrepresented in the catalogue, or verbally by the auctioneer.

The day before the sale you should ensure that your horse is looking its best. If the sale is some distance from your home you may want to stable it overnight to ensure that it is settled when it goes in the ring. This also gives potential purchasers time to view and, if appropriate, to try your horse before the bidding starts. An experienced buyer will be wary of late arrivals, knowing that unless the horsebox broke down en route, the reason for their lateness is that either the horse would not load or the seller did not want to give anyone the chance to view or try it before it entered the sales ring. As a consequence, late arrivals are viewed with some suspicion, and unless bid for by an inexperienced buyer, will command a lower price.

The auctioneers will ask you what sort of price you are hoping your horse will fetch, and whether or not you want to put a reserve on it. If you *have* to sell the horse, no matter what the price, you will not put a reserve on it. However, if there is a price below which you would not consider letting it go, then you must set this as your reserve. Bidders will

AUCTIONEER'S PROBLEM

The biggest problem from the auctioneer's point of view is that sellers tend to put their absolute price on the horse, not their lowest acceptable price. This can mean that out of 200 horses catalogued, only 100 sell.

have no idea of the value you put on your horse so it might leave the ring unsold if it does not reach its reserve. The auctioneers will set their starting price according to the figure you supplied them with, but they may have to lower it in order to get an initial bid. If you are lucky, there may be two or more buyers after your horse and so the bidding will be keen. However, if only one bidder is interested, you might be disappointed. There is always the possibility that you may be approached after the sale by a bidder asking what is the least you will take for your horse. However, this would be classed as a private sale and none of the sale conditions would apply.

When selling a horse at auction, you

have to realise that it is a buyer's market. There are a great many horses to choose from, so if your horse sells for a good price, you either have a good horse or you have been lucky.

Should you observe any likely or actual unnecessary suffering to any horse or pony at a sale, you should report it immediately, in the first instance to the sale's appointed welfare officer or auctioneer, and then to the county council inspector or official veterinary surgeon.

Agencies

These are a fairly new innovation, which do not seem to have caught on very quickly. The idea is much like a computer dating agency, where potential buyers are matched with suitable horses described on a register. The idea is a good one, in that you will only be showing your horse to people who have some indication of its suitability. However, as many buyers do not yet go to these agencies for their requirements, it may take some time before your horse sells. There is normally a registration fee to sellers, with the buyer paying nothing. It will certainly do no harm for your horse to be on a register, but if speed is of the essence then selling by other means will be more appropriate.

SELLING POINTS

When selling a horse you will want to get as much money for it as possible. So how do you sell a horse for the best price to the best home? Everyone's idea of a good horse varies, depending on his/her needs, but there are certain basic requirements that make a horse a desirable purchase:

- A young horse will sell on its looks, its conformation and its pedigree.
- A horse for general hacking will sell on its manners and ride.
- A horse for competitive work will sell on its ability and experience.
- A mare for breeding will sell on her past performance, her conformation and her pedigree.

As the seller you must concentrate on accentuating all your horse's good points. If it has a perfect temperament, make sure you take every available opportunity to show this to the potential customer; likewise if the horse is well schooled.

The most important thing to remember is that 'first impressions count'. It really is worth taking the time to make your horse look good as, no matter how experienced the buyer is, they do not want to have to look through the dirt or rolls of fat in order to see the horse's true potential. If a horse does not make an initial impression, it will be an uphill struggle to get a buyer to take an interest in it, and often he/she will only need

a slight excuse to terminate the viewing. However, if the horse does make a good first impression, a potential buyer will be far more likely to take a keen interest in it, giving it a fair trial.

One of the biggest selling points of any horse is its value, and this is something you have to get just right. Too cheap and people start to think there must be something wrong with the horse; too dear and they simply will not come and look. To help you to set a realistic figure, take a look through the 'for sale' advertisements in your national equestrian magazines. Highlight all those which you feel are similar to your horse, to see what sort of figures are being asked. You may find there is quite

No matter how much you would like your horse to be a top showjumper, you cannot sell him as such if all he has done is jumped round a 3ft course

a range depending upon age, ability, faults and vices and so on, but you should get some idea of the value of your horse.

Again, you must be honest with yourself. No matter how much you would like your horse to be a top showjumper, you cannot sell it as such if all it has done is jump around a 3ft 6in (1m) course. If the horses in the advertisements have won more than your horse, then you will have to set your price lower than theirs; but if your horse has other qualities (perhaps it has show winnings as well) then you can raise the figure accordingly. If this all seems rather confusing, it is because selling *is* a complicated business. No two horses are the same, and at the end of the day a horse is only worth whatever someone is willing to pay for it. As setting the right price is such a crucial factor when selling privately, you will benefit from some unbiased advice from an expert.

TRAINING TO SELL

Having decided upon a suitable price, you need to get your horse ready to sell. The decision to sell a horse often comes only after weeks of debate, so you will probably have plenty of time to prepare it. In the long term this means getting the horse fit, schooled and into good condition; in the short term this means ensuring that it is well groomed and ready for inspection on the appropriate days after the advertisement appears or when it is to go through the sales ring.

As soon as you have made the decision to sell your horse, take a really good look at it. First you should assess its condition, as this will take the longest time to adjust. Is its weight about right, or is it a little too fat or thin? If required, adjust its dietary requirements – but don't overdo it. You don't want the horse to put on more weight than is required or it may become lazy and breathless. Similarly, you don't want it to be so full of energy that it becomes impossible to handle and ride. If you find that it needs slimming down, do this by cutting down on any concentrate part of its ration, not on hay or grass.

Also take a good look at its feet, as nothing is more guaranteed to put a buyer off quickly than poor quality hooves. Obviously, a good diet will show in good horn quality, but you also need to ensure that your horse is shod regularly and well, especially if you have been a little lax over the past months. If you detect a particular problem, have your farrier look at it and start work on it straightaway. It can take six months for a hoof to grow sufficiently for old problems to disappear, so if you have neglected your horse's feet, do not expect the farrier to put them right in one session. While you can put on hoof oil on the morning of the inspection to add to the presentation of your horse, it will do little to improve the condition of the horn or to fool an experienced buyer. However, applying a preparation that contains glycerine will help over a period of time.

You then need to get your horse into shape if it is not in regular work. You will need to work it at least four times a week, starting with plenty of active walking, moving on to trotting and then

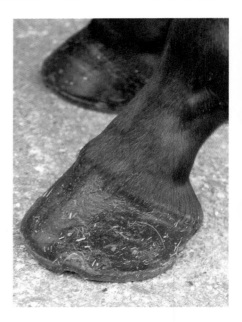

You will need to ensure your horse is shod properly, especially if you have been a bit lapse over the past few months

faster work as it becomes fitter. You don't want to get the horse so fit that it starts to become naughty or too frisky, but it must be active, obedient and enthusiastic when ridden. Make sure you ride it in the area where it will be tried, as well as on the roads or tracks around where you live. Run through 'mock' trials with the horse, working positively on any areas where it shows resistance. Once it is walking, trotting and cantering as well as jumping, if appropriate, on both reins, you cannot ask for more.

Your horse must also show good manners when in hand, and this includes catching it in the field, and handling it in the stable. It is to be hoped that your horse learnt good manners at a young age and will have retained them throughout its time with you. However, if it has been left in the field for a while, it may need a period of 'revision', so that you can be sure it responds obediently to having its feet picked up, being tied up, being groomed and so on. It is also extremely important that the horse walks and trots up in hand when required.

In order to ensure that your horse walks and trots out correctly on the day of viewing, you should take a little time to train it so that it knows exactly what is required of it. To lead it up for a purchaser, stand at its shoulder and lead it smartly away from the buyer in a nice straight line. So you don't wander off the straight line, fix your eye on some point ahead and walk directly towards it; your horse must walk along actively without jogging or without you having to drag it along. If it does either of these two things, you will have to teach it to walk out correctly before you advertise it. With a lazy horse you can hold a schooling whip in your outside hand and flick it towards its hindquarters as you ask it to move on. If it does not respond, give it a tap with the whip until it gets the message. You can calm a horse that keeps jogging by putting on a bridle and taking it for long, quiet walks. This sort of horse will also benefit from being made to stand still in the yard while you chat to your friends so that it gets the idea that, no matter how impatient it is to be off, you will not allow it to do so until you are ready.

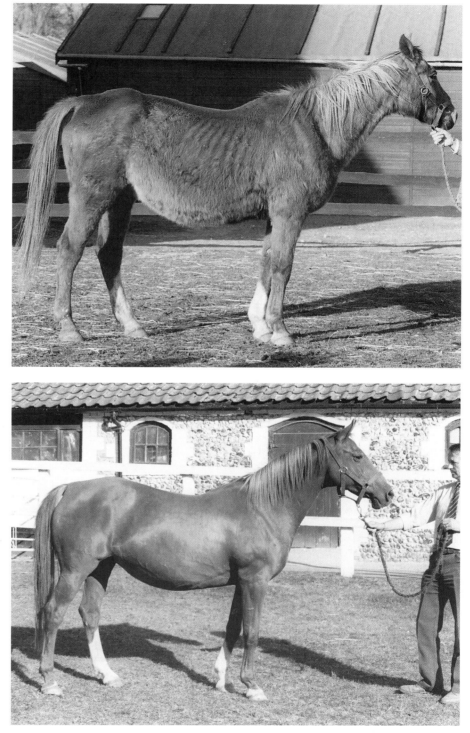

Having decided to sell a horse, first assess his condition, because this will take the longest time to improve. The horse in the top photograph is in extremely poor condition and should never have geen allowed to get into such a state. If this is how your horse looks, then he deserves a new, caring owner and as soon as possible. The bottom picture shows the same horse a few months later having received some proper feeding and management – and if this is the sort of improvement that *you* will need to make in *your* horse, then that is what it will take you: several months, and not just a couple of weeks

When getting your horse into shape, start with plenty of active walking on the roads, moving on to steady trot work, preferably uphill

Having walked away from a buyer, you should then turn the horse *away from you* in a semi-circle and, once back on a straight line, move it briskly into trot towards the buyer. And while the trot should be active, do not go so fast that your horse becomes unbalanced. Also make sure that *you* are up to the task. Nothing looks worse than a trotting horse supporting its handler. Make sure you practise trotting the horse on a loose rein as this will allow it to show its natural action uninhibited by you pulling on its mouth or head. If you hang on to its head, it will turn it towards you which will unbalance the trot, thus hampering its free movement.

PRESENTATION

Here we are back to the initial impression again. When you lead your horse out of its box to stand it up for inspection, it must say immediately, 'Look at me, I'm definitely worth buying.' Take note of where the potential buyer is standing and use this to your advantage. For instance, if your horse has a good, strong neck, face the horse so that the buyer is viewing the non-mane side. But if its neck is a little weak, turn the horse so that the buyer is viewing the mane side. The horse should stand still with its head and neck relaxed in a normal position but showing an interest in its surroundings. Try not to keep a tight hold on the headcollar (halter) or the bridle, but stand away from the horse so that the buyer can get a really good overall impression without you in the picture.

All the horse's legs should be showing, with the two legs furthest from the buyer slightly inside the two nearest to him. The horse should also be standing straight because if it turns its head towards the buyer, this can make the neck appear shorter than it really is. If your horse has really good hocks, trim the tail so that it ends about 2in (5cm)

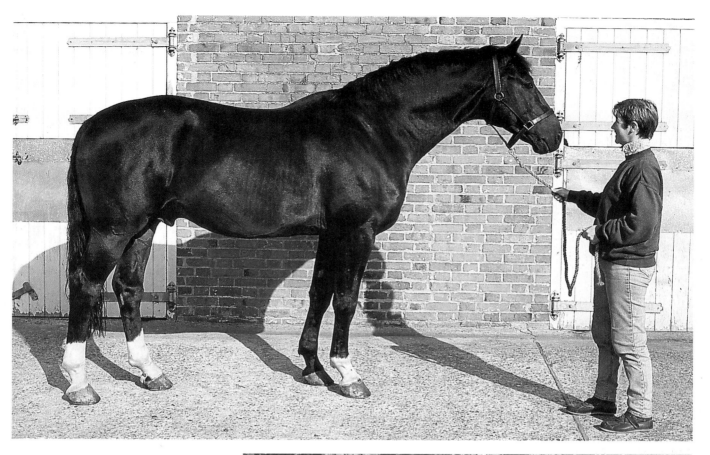

When you lead your horse out of his box you want him to stand up and give the impression of saying: 'Look at me, I'm *definitely* worth buying!'

Compare this photo to the previous one: this horse is not being 'presented' to the potential buyer, and is therefore unlikely to make a good impression

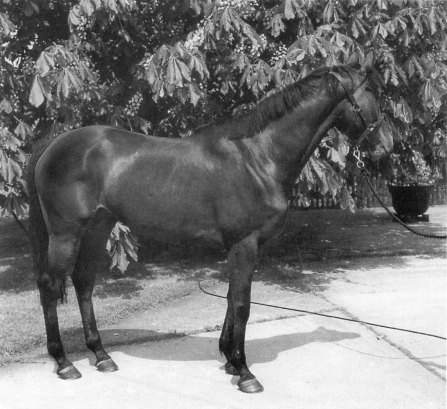

(left) Trim the extra-long whiskers off the horse's face to ensure his head takes on a streamlined appearance

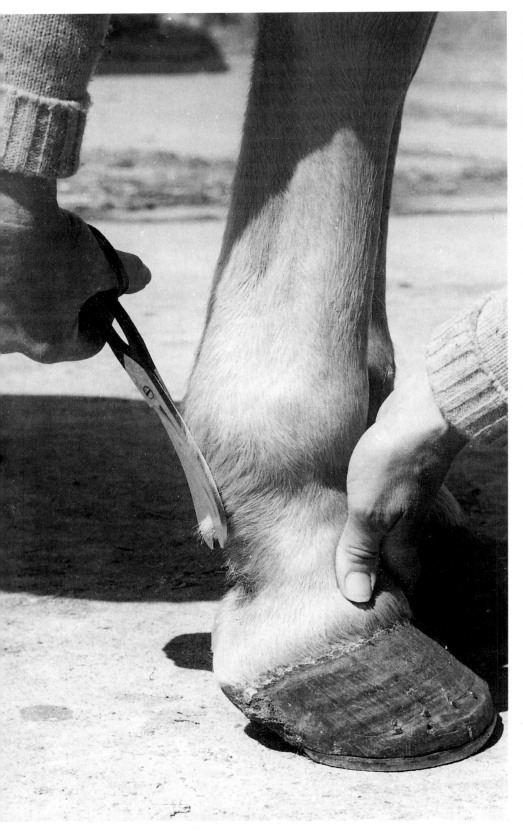

Trimming the excess hair round the legs will help to enhance its appearance and give it a 'clean' look

below the hocks. However, if its hocks are *not* its best asset, you can take the buyer's eye away from them by trimming the tail level with the point of the hocks. None of these things will prevent an experienced buyer from detecting your horse's faults, but they will create a good enough impression so that your horse gets a fair appraisal.

Before anyone comes to view, make sure your horse is well groomed, with its feet picked out and oiled, and its eyes and nose clean. Do not plait it up, but do make sure its mane is neatly brushed on one side of its neck. If the horse has an unruly mane, you will have to 'train' it to lie on one side by leaving it in long plaits for three or four days at a time, before viewing commences. (Do *not* do this the day before someone comes to view the horse, or the mane will look as if it has been permed.)

Make sure any tack you use is clean, supple and well fitting. Also ensure you have all the equipment to hand that you will need; for instance, if your horse is a jumper, make sure the jumps are already set up in the school or paddock.

At the end of the day your horse should sell itself, providing it is in good condition and obviously well behaved – but it still does no harm to try to stamp a favourable initial impression on a buyer's mind.

After the assessment and trial have been concluded, it does no harm to turn the horse out in the presence of the potential buyer, especially if it is the sort to prance about the field showing off.

Finally, do not badger the buyer into giving you a decision there and then. Remember how important it was for *you* to have some time to think about the horse *you* were going to buy? Respect the buyer's need to do this, but do assure him that you will be quite happy to answer any queries he may have over the telephone. If really interested, some buyers will want to return for a second trial, or to bring along an adviser if they did not do so in the first place. Far from viewing this as a nuisance, you should welcome the chance of your horse going to a sensible, caring owner who wants to be certain that it is exactly right for his needs, someone who does not take the attitude that if he makes a mistake he will simply sell the horse on again.

TRIAL PERIOD

Allowing your horse to go out on trial is taking the assessment one step further. While in an ideal world every horse would go out on trial to ensure that it suits the rider or owner, unfortunately we do not live in an ideal world and there are still people who insist on buying horses that are far too much for them to handle. The danger in this, of course, is that, once out of your hands, anything can happen to your horse. It may then be returned to you as unsuitable, with the addition of a few new problems which you will have to sort out before you can advertise it again. My advice is not to allow your horse out on trial unless you are totally satisfied with the level of knowledge of the person who is to have it, and are fully aware of the environment in which it will be kept. Just as you do not want your horse returned because it rears, neither do you want it returned with cuts from barbed wire or kicks from other, unknown horses.

A far better solution is to allow a potential purchaser to come back and try the horse, under your guidance, two or three more times if required. He/she can hack it out, jump it and generally do all he or she might wish to do as if it were already their own. Obviously, if you are selling the horse as a dressage horse, you cannot guarantee that it will be a good jumper, and vice versa, so any trial must be specific to the intended purpose of the potential buyer.

You should, however, beware of time-wasters who simply want to get free rides. Such people can be infuriating, especially if they have prevented other potential customers from viewing your horse. As a rule, you can generally feel that a buyer is serious if he goes to the trouble of having your horse vetted, or lays a non-returnable deposit, unless the horse fails the vet. And if a buyer does neither of these two things, he may be trying to lower the asking price by delaying the time between the advertisement appearing and handing over the money, well aware that you will get less response from an advertisement again. Do not be bamboozled in this way, however. Set him a fair deadline in which to make up his mind, subject to a veterinary examination, especially if you have other interested people wanting to view. If you want to be mercenary about selling your horse, you can simply set a rule that the first one to hand over the money can have it. However, while this may please your bank manager, it is certainly not in your horse's best interests. Once you are happy with a buyer, you can afford to be a little more lenient with him, providing you feel he is genuine and honest.

During the transitional period between viewing and buying, when the buyer may wish to try your horse again or even two more times at your premises, you should have your horse insured for another rider, if it isn't already. While it is on your premises and you are still the legal owner, this is your responsibility. If you do not feel inclined to pay the extra premium (although the sum will be quite insignificant), you can ask the buyer to do so.

Only allow your horse out on trial if you are totally satisfied with the level of knowledge and the ability of the person who is to have it, and only if you are fully aware of the environment in which it is to be kept. In order to ensure that both horse and rider are compatible, and in preference to allowing the horse out on trial, allow the interested buyer to come back and try the horse under your guidance two or three more times; hacking out, or jumping cross country if this is what they require

HONESTY

In the preceding chapters we have seen how much simpler buying and selling horses would be if everyone were honest about their horses and themselves. The best policy for anyone selling a horse is to be totally truthful about it. While you might not make quite as much money as if you try to sell the horse as something it is not, you will not have any of the hassle produced by unhappy buyers. Many owners try to disguise a horse's bad points by avoiding anything that upsets it during a trial. However, it is becoming increasingly difficult to hide a horse's real age or its winnings record, as many countries now have a national horse register with the aim of creating equine identities. The aim of such registers is to bring together all relevant information about a horse's history, including breeding, age, veterinary records, performance records and the performance of related horses. In years to come, all horses will have their own passport, with their own national identification number. This will relate to a central bank of information, and will include the pedigrees of stallions and mares. It will take much of the mystery out of horse buying, leading to a time when any horse without a passport will be treated with suspicion.

Having said that, there is nothing that says you have to point out every lump or bump to a potential owner. Their needs may be very different to yours and a bump here or there, or a little quirk in nature, may not bother them at all. Answer all the potential buyer's questions as honestly as possible, and also make up your own mind as to whether you feel your horse will suit them. If you believe it will not, think very carefully about selling the horse to them, or at least point out your reservations. Two things that you really must mention are any vices, whether stable or ridden, and any permanent health conditions.

Sellers also have another responsibility, and that is to their horse. You should be looking for a fair and caring home, and to this end it is prudent to ask potential purchasers about their level of knowledge, riding skills and the facilities they have for keeping a horse. In fact, as a seller, you might go as far as 'vetting' potential owners. Many buyers will be quite happy for you to see where the horse will be going, others are not so happy about it, perhaps fearing a 'busybody' attitude from you. While you must respect a buyer's wishes and while you do not want to prejudice a sale, at the end of the day you have the right to sell or not to sell a horse to whomsoever you wish. If you get a feeling that the buyer is not going to be a very good owner, you have the right to refuse him, *provided* you have not clearly stated to him in front of witnesses that you intend to sell him the horse.

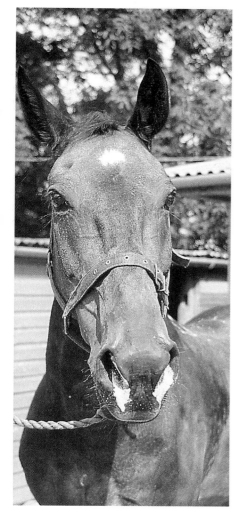

If your horse has a permanent health condition such as COPD, you really must mention it to any potential purchaser

(left) Do you really know the ability, and the level of knowledge, of the person to whom you are selling? Would they know *not* to turn a laminitic pony out onto rich grass, for instance?

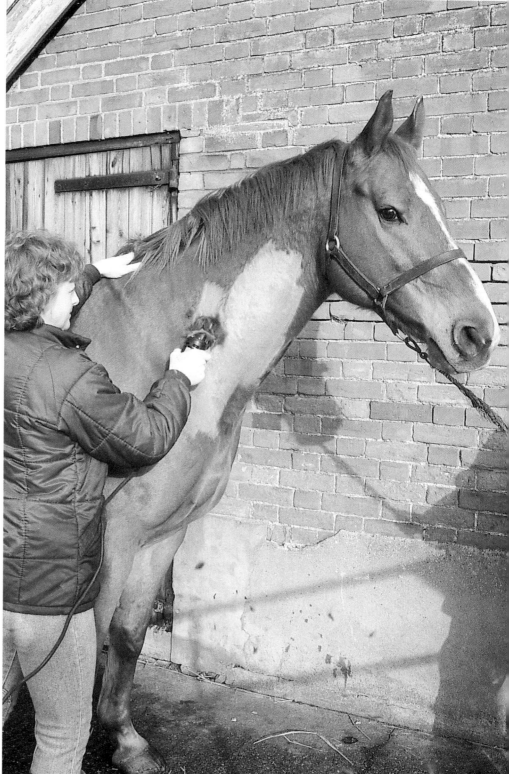

The best policy is to be totally truthful about your horse. For instance, even in summer, do not say your horse is good to clip if you know he most certainly is not. It will only cause you aggravation in the end, and someone may get hurt because of your cover-up

WARRANTIES

You are now on the other side of the coin, as this relates to offering your horse with a warranty. It is amazing how many people buy a horse warranted, only then to try to sell it on without any warranty. Having lived with the horse, they now know that it has a few quirks which, although these do not worry them, they feel may discourage a potential purchaser. You will now appreciate the difficulty in offering a warranty unless pushed to do so. If you are happy to guarantee that your horse is suitable for everything you have discussed with the buyer, and that it has no vices or other peculiarities, you can offer a warranty with some certainty that there will be no comebacks. But do you really know the ability of the person you are selling the horse to? Can you ensure that your horse will not buck him/her off, or stop with him across country simply because he does not have the skill to ride it properly? As you can see, the more you think about it, the more that offering a warranty may begin to cause you some concern.

Similarly, if you put 'good in traffic' and your horse shies at a combine harvester coming along the road, unseating its new rider, you could be held liable. You can try clever wording, such as 'usually good in traffic', but an adroit buyer will soon see through this. It is a sad fact of life that everyone is now careful of litigation, so even the most honest seller is wise to be careful about the wording of warranties. For instance, you should never put 'bombproof' as no horse is *wholly* reliable in *every* situation. In the real world, or course, we all realise that such statements simply mean that the horse has generally proved itself to be almost totally reliable. In the world of law, however, this has to mean that a bomb could literally go off beside the horse and it would still behave itself!

Having considered warranties from both the buyer's and seller's points of view, you can see how difficult it is to reach a satisfactory outcome. The buyer may feel you are trying to 'palm him/her off' with a horse that is not really as described because you are not prepared to put it in writing, and you will feel that you are not prepared to put it in writing simply because you cannot be held liable for the new owner's (not the horse's) ability and knowledge. The best you can do is to assure them quite clearly of your horse's virtues, and if they push the point about a written warranty, explain diplomatically why you are not in favour of offering one. Providing you have been quite honest about your horse, stating both good and bad points, both sides should be quite happy. What you must not do, of course, is try to sell the buyer something your horse is not. If you do so, then you are leaving yourself open to the horse being returned, and worse, being held responsible for any accident or damage that may occur as a result of your cover-up.

SELLING DECISIONS

As previously stated, it is entirely up to you to whom you sell your horse, but if you are a good owner you will be very careful about your horse's prospective new home. There is nothing worse than selling a horse, only for snippets of information to reach you later about how poor it looks or how naughty it is being. If it looks as though someone viewing is going to offer to buy your horse, be very careful about committing yourself to anything other than the asking price before you have had a chance to find out a little more about them. Develop a chatty way of talking to them so that you can elicit information without giving anything away yourself. Blunt questions about their suitability as owners will not be welcomed, whereas general comments from you can often extract some useful replies. Try saying things such as: 'Do you belong to any local riding club?', which may get a response such as: 'Not yet, but I would like to join and have a go at showjumping/dressage.' This will let you know that they are not yet very experienced, but take seriously their responsibility to learn more about riding. On the other hand they may say, 'Oh, I don't bother with lessons any more,' which implies that they think they know it all. If you get an opportunity you could also drop in comments such as: 'Doesn't mucking out take such a long time?' You would hope to get the response, 'Yes, but I get up early and do it before I go to school/work.' Be wary if you get comments such as: 'Oh, I'll just keep him on deep litter as I haven't the time to muck out properly in the mornings.'

Should you get comments that you do not like, try not to show any displeasure or else the buyer will clam up. Get all the information you can, then go indoors, sit down and let off steam over a cup of tea.

PAYMENT

Once you are quite happy to let your horse go to a particular buyer, you can agree the terms of sale. Basically, all that this should consist of is him/her paying for your horse and you handing it over. However, there may be a few complications. He may ask you to keep the horse until he has sorted out livery or had new stables built. In this case, you are fully entitled to ask for livery fees until he collects, or you deliver the horse.

Whatever arrangements you agree to, make sure he pays you in full for your horse before it leaves your premises. If payment is by cash or banker's draft, then you can release the horse immediately. If it is by cheque, hold on to your horse until the cheque clears; unfortunately a cheque can be stopped or lost in the post, or it may be 'bounced' (returned unpaid) because the buyer simply does not have sufficient funds in his account to cover it.

Before the horse leaves your yard, ask the new owners if they mind you staying in touch. Seeing the horse go will be upsetting and stressful for you, no matter how much you thought you had resigned yourself to the idea. However, if you have done all you can to ensure a good home for it, this will make it easier for you to move on with a clear conscience to your next equine partner.

THE END OF THE ROAD

It may be a hard thing to face, but the kindest option for an old, infirm horse may be to have it put down. You will obviously want to discuss this possibility with your vet, but ultimately the responsibility is yours. Finding out that the old horse which you sold in good faith is now being abused, will play far more on your conscience than the trauma of saying goodbye. Destroying a horse is always a distressing experience but the horse's welfare, and thus its quality of life, must always be the prime concern.

Little is ever written about this subject, perhaps because it is such a distressing one, so few people are really aware of the options and what is involved. Perhaps this is one of the reasons why so many people shy away from destroying a horse, preferring to shift the responsibility on to the next owner. However, it is such an important part of the responsibility of horse ownership that I feel it warrants some space in this chapter.

Having a horse put down is called euthanasia, and horses should only be destroyed by a qualified vet or knacker man. Before agreeing to put your horse down, the vet will ask you to sign a consent form, which will probably also require you to acknowledge that you will cover the vet's fees. The process can be quite expensive, so you should get a quote from the vet beforehand. Obviously in an emergency there is no time for any of this preparation, but you will have time where it is a case of putting an end to your old horse's suffering. Before the horse is put down, you will have to make arrangements for the disposal of its carcass, which will incur further costs. Check with your insurance company what cover, if any, is provided for this procedure for old horses.

There are two main ways of putting a horse down: by shooting it with a humane killer, or by injecting lethal doses of drugs. The gun used is a .32 calibre single shot, which is used because of its efficient and fast use in qualified hands. Witnessing this procedure can be a most distressing event, and while you may wish to be with your horse while it draws its last breath, the final moments can leave a disturbing impression upon you. You will hear a very loud bang, immediately followed by the horse collapsing to the ground. There is usually quite a lot of blood loss and jerking, which is a reaction of the nervous system. However, while most unpleasant to witness, you can rest assured that the horse will be dead before it touches the ground and that it will have been largely unaware, if not totally oblivious, of what was happening to it.

No painkillers or sedative drugs should be administered to the horse for some time beforehand if the carcass is destined for animal consumption.

The use of the humane killer is now becoming far less acceptable to horse owners who, these days, often opt for drug-induced euthanasia. The drugs used are those which nowadays are employed as anaesthetics, except that a lethal dose is given. Until recently, these drugs had to be administered through multiple-injected doses, but there is now a single dose which obviously eases the stress on all concerned. Once the dose has been administered, the horse will slip to the ground in between 30 and 60 seconds. Within two or three minutes the actions of the vital organs cease and there is little jerking. As chemicals are used, the horse's body cannot be used for animal consumption; however, the process is far less traumatic for those witnessing it.

Once the horse has been put down, you will have to dispose of the carcass by burial or cremation or by having your local hunt kennelman or knackerman collect it. None is an easy option, but at the end of the day, old or infirm horses deserve better than to be sold on to an unknown fate simply because their owners find it difficult to come to terms with their final responsibility.

SELLING SOLUTIONS

Having just received notification of a place at university, Claire Taylor decided she would have to sell her much loved pony Woody. As she was so busy, Claire sent Woody to her friend Susan who ran a highly respectable sales yard. Susan valued Woody at £500, but Claire said she must sell him before she started university, so they agreed a 'bargain' price of £375 and advertised him at this figure. There was quite a lot of interest and the first people to try him (Sally, and her mum Mrs King) said they liked him very much and would buy him subject to him satisfying a pre-purchase veterinary examination, which he did. They seemed very happy and did not try to haggle over the price.

Mrs King then telephoned Claire direct to ask if they could have Woody on trial for the weekend so they could take him to a show. They also said it would be perfectly acceptable for Claire to come and see where Woody was to be kept. Everything was agreed over the telephone, and Mrs King was to come and collect Woody on Friday evening at six o'clock.

Half an hour later, Mrs King called Claire and started to quibble over the purchase price. Firstly she mentioned that Woody's bottom teeth were worn. (This was true; Woody being a part-bred Dartmoor pony had suffered from 'Dartmoor disease', caused through ponies taking in quantities of granite particles while grazing in the Dartmoor region of the UK.) However, the condition had never affected his ability to eat, or his health in general. Having got nowhere with this grumble, Mrs King then went on to say Woody was unsound because in her opinion one of his hocks was higher than the other. This simply was not true, and the only thing Claire could think of was that at the age of sixteen years, Woody may have been a little stiff on first trotting out. However, even if this was the case it did not seem to have had any influence on the veterinary surgeon's decision to recommend purchase. Claire would not agree to drop the price as she knew Woody was a safe, genuine pony who was being sold at a very good price anyway. Mrs King suggested she be allowed to have the pony for the weekend as arranged, and then they could discuss the final price afterwards.

Claire quickly informed Susan of the complications. Suspecting a possible time-waster, Susan promptly called Mrs King to say there was no chance of her taking the pony as there were other people interested in the pony at the full asking price. Mrs King's final comment before hanging up was 'sell it then!' Obviously Mrs King was not really interested in Woody; she was simply trying to get him for a ridiculous price.

MORAL *When selling a horse or pony ensure both parties are quite happy with the price. As the seller do not invite haggling, but state something that cannot be misinterpreted but needs a positive or negative answer, such as 'and you are quite happy with the price?' If the buyer is, they will say so, and if they are not then you will know not to put off any other potential customers while they try to make up their minds.*

AUCTION AND SALES DIRECTORY

DENMARK

DANSK VARMBLOD
Udkaersvej 15,
Skejby DK-8200
Arhus N
Denmark
Tel: (45) 86109088
Fax: (45) 8610 9160
Date: September – Foal Auction
Location: Vilhelmsborg

DANISH WARMBLOOD SOCIETY
Lundgardsvej 21, 9510 Arden
Tel: (45) 9865 6356
Fax: (45) 9856 6160
Contact: Jan Pederson
Date: September – Foal Auction
Location: Arden

FRANCE

UNIC
22, Rue De Penthievre, 75008 Paris
Tel: (331) 45 62 00 52
Fax: (331) 42 25 96 75

1 FENCES SALES
Date: August – Pompadour Sale;
September – 7th Elite Breeding Stock
and Sport Horse Sale (brood mares,
foals, yearlings, 2 and 3 year olds)
Location: Espace Marchel Rozier, 77590
Bois-le-Roi (near Fontainbleau)
Contact: FENCES, La Cour Bonnet,
14700 Falaise
Tel: (33) 31 90 93 24
Fax: (33) 31 40 12 26

2 DEAUVILLE SALE
Date: October – showjumping sale
for the National Class horses for the
horse Expo show occasion
Location: The Horse Expo Lancel,
Deauville
Contact: UNIC

3 POITERS SALE
Date: November – Sport horses and
breeding stock
Contact: OGCS, 1 Route de Chauvigny,
86550 Mignaloux, Beauvoir
Tel: (33) 49 46 25 61

4 BIARRITZ SALE
Date: November – Anglo Arab sale
Contact: ANAA
Tel: (33) 61 75 41 49
Fax: (33) 61 75 41 40

GERMANY

**WESTFALISCHES
PFERDESTAMMBUCH EV**
PO BOX 460107, D-48072 Münster
Tel: (49) 251 3280981
Fax: (49) 251 3280924
Date: August – Foal Auction;
October – Westphalian riding horses
Location: Münster

TRAKEHNER VERBAND
Postfach 2729, D-24517 Neumunster
Tel: (49) 4321 90270
Fax: (49) 4321 902719
Dates:
1 September Riding horses, Brood
mares and foals
2 October- Graded and non-graded
stallions,
broodmares and foals
3 April – Riding horses auction
Location:
1 Kloterhof Medingen,
Niedersachsen
2 Neumunster, Holstenhalle

**LANDESVERBAND BAYERISCHER
PFERDERZÜCHTER EV**
Landshamer Strasse,
11 81929 München
Tel: (49) 89 9269613
Fax: (49) 89 907405
Date: March
Location: München Olympia Reithalle

**VERBAND SER ZUCHTER DES
HOLSTEINER PFERDES EV**
Westerstrassse 93, D-25336 Elmshorn
Tel: (49) 4121 93729
Fax: (49) 4121 93629
Date: November
Location: Neumunster, Holstenhalle

PFERDEZUCHTVERBAND BERLIN
Hauptgestüt 10,
16845 Neustadt, Dosse, BRD
Date: October
Location: Brandenburgisches
Landgestüt

ANKUMER OPEN SALES GMBH
Am Borgberg 3
D-49170 Hagen aTW
Tel: (49) 5401 9430
Fax: (49) 5401 9417
Date: October, April
Location: Sportscentre Ankum

**PERFORMANCE SALES
INTERNATIONAL**
Am Borgberg 3
D-49170 Hagan aTW
Tel: (49) 5401 9819
Fax: (49) 5401 9417
Date: December
Location: Sportscentre Ankum

**VERBAND HESSISCHER
PFERDEZUCHTER EV**
Pfderdezentrum Alsfeld, AN der
Hessenhalle 5, D-36304 Alsfield
Tel: (49) 663 172011
Fax: (49) 663 172016
Contact:Klaus Biedenkopf
Date: October, March

**PFERDERZUCHTERVERBAND
RHEINLAND-PFALZ SAAR EV**
Pfderzentrum,
68716 Standenbuhl
Tel: (49) 6357 897
Fax: (49) 6357 1501
Date: March
Location: Laudgestüt Zweibrucken

AÜKTIONSBURO VECHTA
Reiterwaldstadiojn,
D-49377 Vechta in Oldenberg
Tel: (49) 441 3401
Date: October
Location: Vechta

VERBAND DER ZUCHTER UND
FREUNDE DES OSTPPREUSSISCHEN
WARMBLUTCHER DES TRAKEHNER
ABSTAMMUNG EV
Max Eyth-Strasse 10, D 24537
Neumunster
Tel: (49) 4321 90272
Fax: (49) 4321 902719
Dates: September, October
Location: Klasterhof, Medingen

VERBAND HANNOVERSCHER
WARMBLUTZUCHER EV
Lindhooper Str, D-27283 Verden/Aller
Tel: (49) 4321 6730
Fax: (49) 4321 67312
Dates: Held throughout the year
Location: Neidersachsenhalle,
D-27283 Verden

THE NETHERLANDS

BORCULO FOAL AUCTION
c/o Kulsdom 9, 7274 EG Geesteren
Tel: (31) 5458 1259
Fax: (31) 5458 1271
Date: August
Location: Terrein Kerkemeijer,
Ruurloseweg, Borculo

UNITED KINGDOM

ANGLO EUROPEAN STUDBOOK LTD
PO Box 61, Tunbridge Wells, Kent
Tel: (01892) 864894
Date: October
Location: Addington Manor, Bucks

THE NATIONAL LIGHT HORSE
BREEDING SOCIETY (H.I.S)
96 High Street, Edenbridge,
Kent TN8 5AR
Tel: (01732) 866277
Fax: (01732) 867464
Date: September
Includes the CLEVELAND BAY HORSE
SOCIETY SALE and the IRISH
DRAUGHT HORSE SOCIETY SALE
Location:
1 Three Counties Showground,
Malvern, Worcs
2 Great Yorkshire Showground,
Harrogate, Yorks

RUSSEL BALDWIN AND BRIGHT
MARKETS
16, Castle Street, Hay on Wye,
Herefordshire HR3 5DF
Tel: (01497) 820622
Fax: (01497) 821435
Date: September
Location: Three Counties
Showground, Malvern, Worcs

MESSRS J.P. BOTTERILL
AUCTIONEERS
Flaxton, York YO6 7PZ
Tel: (01904) 468240/616
Fax: (01904) 468622
Date:
September – Addington CDI Elite
Dressage Sale
November – Addington International
Sale (foals, stallions, mares etc)
May (Easter weekend) – International
Sale (three years old and upwards)
Location: Addington Manor

CLEVELAND BAY HORSE SOCIETY
York Livestock Centre, Murton
York YO1 3UF
Tel: (01904) 489731
Fax: (01904) 489782
Date: September

Location: Great Yorkshire Showground,
Harrogate, North Yorkshire

THE BRITISH HANOVERIAN
SOCIETY
Midwinter Lodge, Mannshill,
Bossingham, Canterbury,
Kent, CT4 6ED
Tel: (01227) 709357
Contact: Alan Akehurst
Date: October – Hanoverian Breed
Show.
Location: Stoneleigh

BRITISH BAVARIAN WARMBLOOD
ASSOCIATION
Sittyton, Straloch, Newmachar,
Aberdeen AB2 0RP
Contact: Christa Jeffery
Tel: (01651) 882226
Fax: (01651) 882313
Date: May

UNITED STATES OF AMERICA

The situation in the USA is rather
different in that each state has its
own scheme of auctions and sales.
Further information may be obtained
from the United States Department of
Agriculture, Riverdale, Maryland.

AUSTRALIA AND NEW ZEALAND

Information may be obtained from
the following addresses:

THE AUSTRALIAN EQUESTRIAN
TRADE ASSOCIATION
PO Box 88, Balgowlah, NSW 2093

THE EQUESTRIAN FEDERATION OF
AUSTRALIA
Lojon House, Royal Agricultural
Showground, Paddington, NSW 2021

INDEX